THE PUSHKIN TRUST

Voices

25 YEARS OF THE PUSHKIN TRUST

Acknowledgements

Pushkin Anniversary Committee

The Duchess of Abercorn
Helen Slattery Cannon
Lynn Greer
Shiela McCaul
Anne McErlane
Denise Mullan
John Quinn
Phoebe Simpson

Illustrator

Gordon D'Arcy

Photography

Alan Boyd
(33, 67, 73, 77, 86, 99, 101, 115, 121)

Kelvin Boyes
at Press Eye Photography
(137)

Helen Slattery Cannon
(25, 29, 35, 51, 79, 90, 113, 119, 141, 155)

Paraig Cannon
(69, 139)

Harry Cook
(125)

Lynn Greer
(17, 47, 59, 147, 149)

Bobbie Hanvey
(178)

Darren Kidd
at Press Eye Photography
(9, 160)

Alan Lewis
Photopress, Belfast
(127)

Deirdre McKay
(49, 85)

Kathryn Nelson
(20, 105)

Roisin Nugent
(15, 129, 145)

Éamonn Ó Murchú
(43)

Richard Pierce
(89)

Patricia Ronan
(63)

Professor Paul Seawright
(143)

Phoebe Simpson
(37, 39, 55, 65, 95, 107, 133, 135, 151, 153, 157)

Máire Uí Mhaicín
(109)

**The Pushkin Trust is very grateful to the following authors
and publishers for permission to reprint:**

Roald Dahl
The BFG, Jonathan Cape Ltd.
The Wonderful Story of Henry Sugar and six more, Penguin Books Ltd.

Mark Patrick Hederman
The Boy in the Bubble   Education as Personal Relationship, Veritas

Every effort has been made to trace copyright holders.
The publishers apologise for any errors or omissions.

Contents

The Song of the Firebird	Sacha Abercorn	9
Who is Pushkin?	Professor Marcus Wheeler	11
The Pushkin Trust in Ireland		12
Source	Seamus Heaney	14
Pushkin	Sacha Abercorn	16
Carrablagh Gardens	Cormac Rogers	18
Pushkin – An Inspiration to All	Kathryn Nelson	19
Writing Matters	Maura Melia	22
A Sick Cow	Neal Coll	24
Summer Night Haiku	Margaret Boucher	26
Taking Flight	Mairéad Ennis	27
The Power of Pushkin	Larry Monteith	28
In the Beginning	Shiela McCaul	30
My Leafy Protector	Peter McGettigan	32
Letting Creativity Flow	Alice Ring	34
My Dad	Nicola Fyffe	35
The Art of the Pushkin Dance	Jenny Elliott	36
Vivid Childhood Memories	Gráinne O'Kane	38
Winter's Wrath	Anna Murray	40
Pushkin … Building Smashing Towers	Frank Galligan	42
Amazing Roots	Mark Gallagher	44
Drowning in the Imagination	John McDaid	45
John Moriarty Thinks of Pushkin and the Children of Ireland	OR Melling	46
Opening Windows of Wonder	Colm Harte	48
The Inestimable Value of Creative Writing	Joan Newmann	50
Hippo	Ronan Geraghty	52
Excavating the Crevices of Memory	Anne Fitzgerald	53
Pushkin's Gift to the Children of Ireland	Alan Boyd	54
The Bog Song	Susan Doherty	56
The Pushkin Grail Quest	Lindsay Clarke	58
The Beach	Gerard Connolly	60
Dear Aisling	John Quinn	62
'The Pushkin Species'	Valerie Murphy	64
Pushkin Magic	Jess Webb	66
Thoughts of a Snowdrop Bulb	Emma Ward	68

A Night at the Niland – Pushkin's 15th Anniversary .... Anita Robinson 70

Partners in Education Programme – A Lecturer's Perspective .... Dr. Michael Flannery 72

Leonard, Parzival and Pushkin .... Roy Arbuckle 74

Inspiring Educators .... Anne McErlane 76

New Roots .... Amanda Gallagher 78

A New-Found Faith .... Paraig Cannon 80

Let Some Sunlight In .... Molly Goyer Gorman 81

Symbol of Hope –A Visit to Russia .... Shiela McCaul 82

Dear Denise .... Alison Turner 84

The Russian Dimension .... Antonina Kosjakina 86

The Tale of Pushkin House .... Richard Pierce 88

Cúchulainn goes to Moscow and finds Kolobok .... Peter Heaney 92

A View from Russia .... Anastasya Skoromnaya 94

A Memorable Visit to Pushkin's Petersburg .... Marie Heaney 96

My Pushkin Memory .... Oksana Pashyan 98

How Can I Keep from Singing? .... Helen Slattery Cannon 100

Survival .... Curtis Burgess 102

The Mild Winter .... Cathy Gormley 103

The Simple Truth .... Mark Patrick Hederman 104

The Classroom Visit .... Pearl Stewart 106

'Where I come from' .... Duyen Jones 108

At Annaghmakerrig's Door .... Kitty Hughes 110

The Redwood Tree .... Lynn Greer 112

The Fire Within .... Betty Orr 114

Silence .... Alan Laird 116

The Symbol of Hope .... Ann Buckley 117

Sycamore Seeds .... Gráinne Toomey 118

A Path to Sound .... Deirdre McKay 119

So Many Memories .... Mary O'Kane 120

The Fish .... Dianne Smyth 122

My Wish for Pushkin .... Hilda Quin 124

A 'Coming of Age' Celebration –The Waterfront Hall – 7th June 2005 .... Sue Michaelson 126

The Roots of Spring .... Orla Duignan, Cara Gilliland, Jack Kelly 128

Journeying from Connectivity to Creativity through Pushkin .... Paddy Madden 130

The Right Word .... Adrian Rice 132

My Place .... James McCollum 134

Enchantment Reigned .... Gordon D'Arcy 136

Drúcht an tSaoil .... Máire Andrews 138

Mum .... Harry Grace 139

The All-Embracing Spirit of Pushkin .... Kate Newmann 140

Reflections .... Tom Morrow 142

Colours .... Chiara Fiorentini, Aoife Duggan, Tamika Bradley ... 144

The Pushkin Challenge .... Jaki McCarrick 146

Cycles .... Claire McMenamin 148

Partners in Education – A Tutor's Perspective ... Steve Batts 150

Roots .... Eimear Rogers 152

A Pushkin Moment .... Tom Mullins 154

Redemption .... Michael Longley 156

Pushkin Patrons and Judges .... Introduction 161

Maeve Binchy 162

Dermot Bolger 164

Sandy Brownjohn 166

Lindsay Clarke 168

Roald Dahl 170

Polly Devlin 172

Gabriel Fitzmaurice 174

Aubrey Flegg 176

Brian Friel 178

Frank Galligan 180

Carlo Gébler 182

Marie Heaney 184

Seamus Heaney 186

Frieda Hughes 188

Ted Hughes 190

Benedict Kiely 192

Joan Lingard 194

Michael Longley 196

William Trevor 198

Martin Waddell 200

Gerard Whelan 202

Pushkin Judges 204

Pushkin Trust Funders 206

The Song of the Firebird

As we open the pages of this book celebrating the 25th Anniversary of the Pushkin Trust, a chorus of voices rings out loud and clear! They are the voices of children, of teachers, of artists and of environmentalists – everyone who has been involved in working with the creative spirit in schools in Ireland over the past twenty-five years – and they all sing in unison!

Their song is a kind of hymn celebrating the power of the imagination to transform and to heal and it resounds with enthusiasm and an eagerness to live. But this song was born, in the dark days of the Troubles in Northern Ireland, out of the 'cry of the child' – a cry of terror that I heard not only in my own child, but in every other 'child' – the 'child' that lives deep within us all.

The sense of outrage that this awoke in me combined with a horrifying sense of powerlessness as to what could be done, as we lived through an eternity of death and destruction, bombs and bullets, left me speechless.

Then, as if like a feather falling gently from the sky above, a magical moment happened. A large gathering of people from Russia, from differing backgrounds and ideologies came together at Luton Hoo, my grandmother's home, to commemorate the life and work of my great, great, great grandfather, Alexander Pushkin. The voice of this great poet, who spoke for the very soul of Russia, transcended all barriers, all borders. For a brief enchanted moment, poetry, music and song achieved what seventy years of diplomacy had failed to do and our hearts took wing!

It was as if I had been touched by this magical feather and I instantly realised that I must carry its message safely back with me to my home in Northern Ireland to see how it might help the children of our troubled land to find a voice and tell us their story in writing.

Over these past twenty-five years not only have children in schools begun to find a voice but likewise those who are responsible for their growth to full potential – their teachers. We now realise that only by the nurturing of the creative spirit in both the child and the child within the adult will we be able to reclaim our Birthright – to find our voice and to sing the song of our soul – the song of the Firebird arising from the ashes.

May this song be heard far and wide – its time has come!

Sacha Abercorn

Sacha Abercorn

A page from Pushkin's working notebooks

Who is Pushkin?

He was one of those giants of the nation's culture who can be called masters of our hearts and minds for all seasons. His poetry was full of freedom, sunshine, love, lively boldness, Russian irony, challenge, pride of intellect, and charity towards the weakness of spiritual misfortunes of the under-privileged.

Yury Bondarev (1987)

It would be difficult to better this evocation of Pushkin, composed, on the 150th anniversary of his death, by the Russian writer. Unlike many tributes, whose hyperbole would have evoked derision in the poet himself, this one hits exactly the right emotive and descriptive pitch. For the Pushkin here described is not unrecognisable from the boy whose first-year school report characterised him as "loquacious, witty, noticeably good-natured but very quick-tempered and flippant."

Pushkin, as a schoolboy at the new Tsarskoe Selo Lycée, was emotionally immature but, in his conduct and in his early poems, precociously sophisticated- a quality which made him a magnet to his peers but also attracted the approving notice of a slightly older group of Russians. These, having fought the war of 1812 against Napoleon, had reacted sharply to the subsequent political and cultural clampdown imposed by the Emperor, Alexander I. Pushkin's ambivalent attitude to authority, especially in the spheres of art, morals, politics and religion, has been attributed by some to his strange genealogy. While his father's family were long-established Russian noblemen, his great-grandfather on his mother's side was an Ethiopian, Ibrahim Hannibal, who had been procured in Constantinople in 1706 by an agent of Peter the Great, brought to Russia and later rewarded handsomely for service to his adoptive country. Arina Rodionovna, his famous nanny, has been identified as the primary source of Pushkin's love of Russian folklore. He learnt from her a love of nature and the simple, direct speech of the people which he used, where appropriate, in his own writing in preference to the stilted language preferred in literary circles in Russia at that time.

But what best describes Pushkin's evolution from blasé adolescent to loved and respected victim of a duelist's pistol is the journey through his own literary composition. His poem *The Gypsies* exposes flaws in the Romantic quest for unrestricted freedom and the cult of the "noble savage" which might have been his own temptations in youth; his "novel," composed in neo-classical verse, *Yevgeny Onegin*, presents a thinly-disguised critique of amoral pleasure-seekers such as he himself must have been; in his "Shakespearean" drama *Boris Godunov* and the novel *The Captain's Daughter,* he explores controversial episodes in Russian history to puncture the complacency of official self-assurance; *The Bronze Horseman,* perhaps his finest long poem, balances a paean to the new imperial Russia of Peter the Great with a plea for those "little" people crushed by Peter's dictatorial machine. Pushkin is the embodiment of a principle: that the writer creates what he or she writes, but the writing process, in turn, recreates the person of the writer.

Professor Marcus Wheeler

The Pushkin Trust in Ireland

1987

Inspired by Alexander Pushkin, the **Pushkin Prizes Project was established** by The Duchess of Abercorn. The project aimed to "unite children and adults in the common bond of creativity which transcends all the factors which might otherwise divide them."

In the first year there were **eight schools involved**; four in Co. Tyrone and four in Co. Donegal, four Catholic and four Protestant schools, representing the **cross-border, cross-community dimension** to the project.

1990

A Symbol of Hope, the first anthology of children's writing, was published. There were **nineteen schools** in the programme. **A trip to Russia** was organised for teachers and children in the project and for previous prizewinners. Its aim was to establish links with the land of Pushkin. UTV documented this visit.

1991

A return trip was made to Ireland by students and teachers from Russia. This was a rich cultural exchange and cemented the links between Ireland and Russia.

1993

The Summer School in Creative Writing for Teachers was established. This was designed to support and inspire teachers in the role of 'teacher-as-writer.' The first **Residential Training Conference for Teachers** was held in November.

1994/1995

The Pushkin project had grown to encompass **fifty schools** in the annual creative writing programme, with a broader geographical spread.

1996

Opening Doors, a second anthology of children's writing, was published. For the first time **four Russian schools took part** in the writing competition. **A trip to St. Petersburg** took place.

1997

A celebration of the **10th Anniversary of the Pushkin Prizes** was held in Trinity College, Dublin. **Seamus Heaney** was the guest of honour for the evening and gave a reading of his poems. A specially commissioned film *The Spirit of Pushkin* was shown on BBC Northern Ireland.

1998

The first **Summer Camp of the Imagination** was held at Baronscourt for children, their parents and teachers. This new departure represented an expansion in the focus of the experiential work, **encompassing the creative arts** in general while using the **environment** to inspire the creative endeavours. An **Irish-medium section** in the creative writing programme was established.

1999

Eager we are to Live, the third anthology of children's writing, was published and launched by the then **Minister for Education, Mr. Michéal Martin** and **Seamus Heaney** at the Hugh Lane Gallery, Dublin.

2000

The Partners in Education Programme was established which involved student teachers and their lecturers from all the Colleges of Education in the Republic.

The **regionalisation** of the work of the Pushkin Trust began with the appointment of five **Regional Leaders**. Based on the Summer Camp of the Imagination, **Baronscourt Days**, became a feature of the programme during the Spring term.

2001

Snow in Summer, an anthology of teachers' writing was published and launched by the then **Minister of Education, Mr. Martin McGuinness** and **Pushkin Patron** and poet **Michael Longley** at the Verbal Arts Centre in Derry.

2002

The **Creative Writing Programme concludes**. More than **20,000 children** had taken part in the programme over fifteen years with **twenty-eight out of thirty-two counties** having been represented in the schools' programme. The **15th Anniversary of the Pushkin Trust** is celebrated with a gathering at the Niland Gallery, Sligo, when the special guest speaker was **Seamus Heaney**.

2003

The **Pushkin Awards** were established, celebrating inspired learning. In this pilot phase twenty schools were involved. **A trip to Russia** was organised to commemorate the 300th Anniversary of the founding of St. Petersburg. At the annual commemoration at Pushkin's Lycée, The Duchess of Abercorn read two poems from *Feather from the Firebird*, her collection of prose poems.

2005

'A Coming of Age' Celebration was hosted at the Waterfront Hall in Belfast with special guests, the **Pushkin Patrons, Seamus Heaney** and **Michael Longley**. This departure marked the scaling back of the schools' programme to focus on the development of the Pushkin ideologies in the arenas of business and the wider community.

2010

The Inspiring Educators' Programme was established, focussing on the personal and professional development of the teacher and the development of a whole-school approach to the promotion of creativity.

2012

25 years of the Pushkin Trust in Ireland was celebrated at the Grand Opera House, in Belfast with special guest performer, **Katie Melua**, who composed *The Story's Magic* for the occasion. She shared the stage with children from north and south.

A Mid-Summer Celebration was hosted in Baronscourt in June to bring together Pushkin facilitators and educators and, in November, The Duchess of Abercorn hosted a **Gala Evening** in Titanic Quarter to celebrate the work of the Pushkin Trust.

2013

Voices, a commemorative publication to mark twenty-five years of the Pushkin Trust in Ireland is launched by the singer-songwriter and first Pushkin prizewinner, **John McDaid**, at the Verbal Arts Centre in Derry.

Source

Twenty-five years on, and the theme of the Pushkin Trust's activities this year is 'Source', one of the most promising words in the language. All of its immediate associations are positive. From a source a well springs, a river flows, a fountain plays, an idea arrives. Once upon a time-around Shakespeare's time – it even meant 'the act of rising on a wing, on the part of a hawk or other bird.'

Since the Pushkin idea was turned into Pushkin activity, good things have continued to flow from that source. Thanks to the creative writing programmes sponsored by the Trust, thousands of students have risen on the wing of a talent they never realised they had. Completing a piece of imaginative work that marks the inner self with a little growth ring, and these intimate transformations are in turn the source of a new confidence. A new trust is conjured within individuals and transmits itself like a live current into the group.

In an ecstatic poem by John of the Cross, the saint celebrates the Divine Presence as 'all sources' source and origin,' and it can be said that there is also a wonderful confluence of spirit and vision and action in the case of the Pushkin movement, the schools finding inspiration in their teachers, the teachers in the vision of The Duchess of Abercorn, the Duchess in the experience and example of her great ancestor, the poet Alexander Pushkin.

I once wrote a poem about a water diviner, a man who can locate the hidden spring and release a hidden supply. I meant the diviner to be read as a figure of the poet or artist, somebody who can find his or her own way to realities and revelations. When, for example, Sacha divined a meaning for Ireland, north and south, in the life and work of Pushkin much human potential was released. His life revealed the value of story at an early age in the development of a creative person and the good energies released into the world by such an individual.

The Schools' Programme is based on such a faith: it is a cross-curricular, cross-community and cross-border project, opening classrooms to authors and artists and outings to Baronscourt. The branches of the Pushkin tree now spread wide and in its shade the work of 'Inspiring Education' proceeds. It grows and it spreads – schools in Russia, a training college in Moscow are now part of the conversation – so that a quarter century after the source was located, we can rejoice that the influence of the Duchess, Pushkin's descendant, and the Pushkin movement in general are in full flow.

Seamus Heaney
Pushkin Patron

Pushkin

A coal of burning ebony, passionate fire uncontainable,
destined to burn a trace through the strictures of tsardom.

Pushkin was happiest writing from the womb of his bed.

I see him now, sitting by her at the hearth. The night closes
in as she tells him the stories of his land – wolves and
witches take form in the flickering firelight.

He laughs and teases with rapier agility.

Drawn like a moth to the flame of the feminine. The quill
that he held between thumb and forefinger like a feather
from the breast of the firebird.

Too hot a coal to hold for long, he burnt through the very
fabric of his time.

Sacha Abercorn

Carrablagh Gardens

Unicorns,
leprechauns,
pegasus
and dragons fly
through this
mythical world
of magical creatures.
Rhododendrons
sway in the wind.
Flowers bloom.
Bees pollinate
to their hearts content.
They buzz off
into their honeycombed nest
where the queen casts
her spell over
Carrablagh Gardens.
We buzz,
billions of bees
pollinating.
As we aim
for the dartboards
of nature.

The unicorns
gallop through
the walled garden.
Dragons fly by the pond.
The leprechaun
jigs by the polytunnel.
And that's Carrablagh Gardens.
For me to know
And waiting for you to find out.

Cormac Rogers
Pupil

Pushkin – An Inspiration to All

When I work within the natural environment I endeavour to avoid the permanent and use instead time-based artworks. This is for ecological reasons since I am motivated to ensure that the footstep of the work does not destroy the beauty of the landscape. To reinforce this philosophy I use wherever possible materials that are natural and are therefore in themselves part of the landscape. I also attempt to inspire and attune the children and adults with whom I work, to the beauty and dynamism of nature. Artworks from my own practice also draw inspiration from the natural environment.

Concept is also an integral part of my professional practice. Currently my work is scientific and mathematical, looking particularly at the beauty of numbers, and the elemental simplicity of line. Yet even here the natural environment plays a vital role since primarily my work strives to elucidate the aesthetic beauty of both mathematics and that of nature.

I believe working within a conceptual framework allows for a shift in perception and validates many forms of composition and representation. It is this continual reframing of stylistic dialogue, as well as the natural environment, that unifies my own practice with my work with the Pushkin Trust. Yet primarily it is Her Grace, The Duchess of Abercorn, who is inspirational to the visual art that I facilitate within the Pushkin Trust. She annually contextualises the environment thematically and *The Living Tree* was just one of her wonderful stimuli for creative thought and ideas:

> *Since the dawn of time, Ireland has been a land of myth and legend, of magical fairytale and imaginative thinking.*
>
> *The time has now come for this legacy not only to be re-envisioned, but to be embodied in each one of us. May 'The Living Tree' become the centre point of this verdant land – a new Garden of Eden full of young saplings, well rooted in the earth, stretching upwards and outwards to their fullest potential, living in harmony from the very core of their beings. In this lies the Ireland of the future.*

*"When Pushkin came to our school
it turned our whole class around."*

I believe, through the Pushkin Trust, every child is shown that there is nothing more important than the natural environment. As Joseph Bharat Cornell writes:

In today's world of overpopulation and high consumption, it is essential that we make an effort to keep children in touch with the earth: its natural rhythms, the changing seasons, its beauty and mystery. In fact, nothing will suffice, short of teaching children to love nature, to love life.

The Baronscourt days are filled with this exemplar, yet what makes the Pushkin Trust so truly remarkable is that the natural and the artistic worlds have been woven together so beautifully to create a warm tangible space that is an inspiration to all.

Kathryn Nelson
Visual Artist

Footnote

Joseph Bharat Cornell, *Sharing Nature with Children*, Exley Publications, 1997.

Writing Matters

It was Friday morning in Annaghmakerrig; the culmination of a week when friendships were forged, anxieties were calmed and appetites for the writing process whetted. This was the morning when we would all share our written offerings.

We were an anxious gathering. We were feeling the effects of the late night celebration of the previous evening but more significant than that however, was the prospect of sharing our pieces with an audience of our peers and our tutors. Some of us had never dared to write personal pieces before. And now we were to read them aloud?

The session began. There were memories from childhood, pen portraits of significant figures, stories created from pictures, haikus revealing the succinct power of brevity. Each one was greeted with encouragement – a smile, a nudge, a clap and after each offering there was appreciative applause, acknowledging the talent or the effort. And then Maureen Boyle stood to read her piece:

Cut My Lace
Cut my lace and I will sing
Cut my lace and I will dance
Cut my lace and I will weep
Cut my lace and I will *live* again
Cut my lace.

There is a land far, far away –
far from hope and far from reason,
where ministries of Vice and Virtue rule
and little girls can't go to school.

Cut my lace and I will sing
Cut my lace and I will dance
Cut my lace and I will weep
Cut my lace and I will *read* again
Cut my lace.

Voices torn out of throats –
unspooled trophies hung on poles.
In the edicts of this land
only clerics have a hand.

Cut my lace and I will sing …

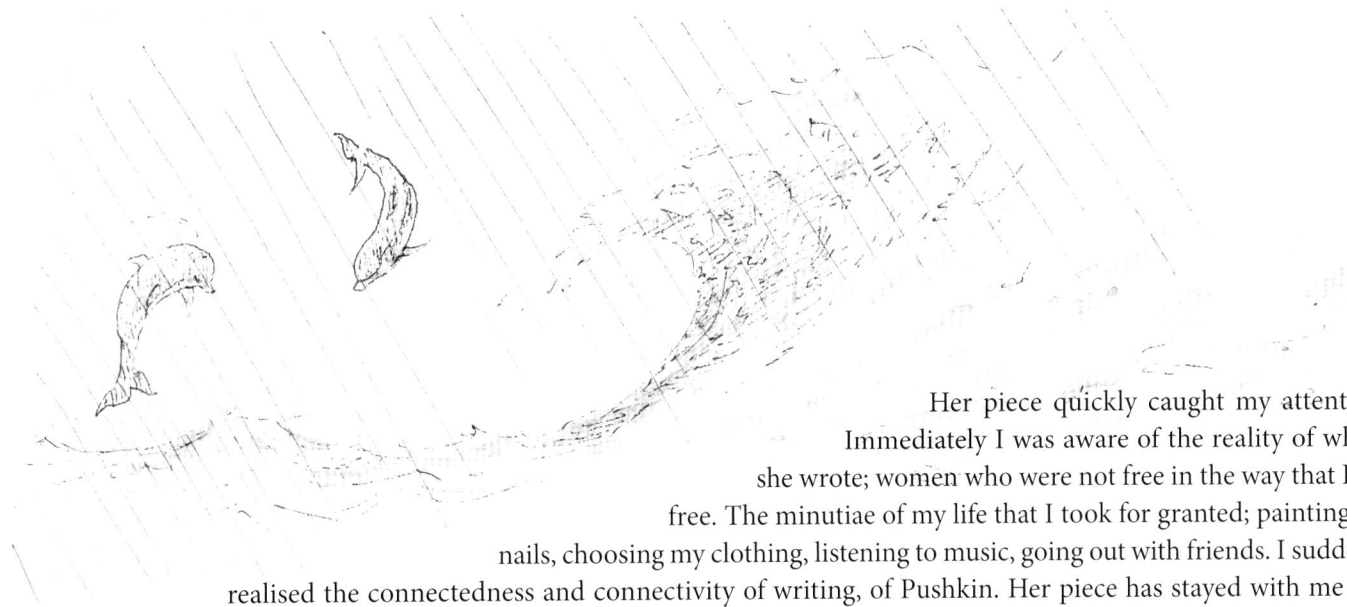

Her piece quickly caught my attention. Immediately I was aware of the reality of which she wrote; women who were not free in the way that I am free. The minutiae of my life that I took for granted; painting my nails, choosing my clothing, listening to music, going out with friends. I suddenly realised the connectedness and connectivity of writing, of Pushkin. Her piece has stayed with me as I listen to news from around the world; as I picture the lives of women in Middle Eastern countries.

The written word has the power to evoke and awaken awareness; the power to cause others to identify; the power to give a voice to the silent. Writing matters. It is important to give a voice to those who would otherwise be silenced. Pushkin has been doing that for twenty-five years. It has caused us to listen, to take heed, to encourage, to give expression to, to applaud, to dream.

Maura Melia
Retired Teacher and Pushkin Regional Leader, 2002–2007

"It is powerful to be spoken to in a different and more idealistic language and one that tells you what you do matters and is important."

A Sick Cow

Thump – Thump – went the familiar thud of Daddy's wellies as he kicked them off outside the kitchen door before entering.

"Something's wrong with that black Friesian, she's not getting to the nuts. Not strong enough I suspect."

I vaguely remembered the birth of that same cow – a lovely glossy calf she was too.

"I'll go and look at her with you later," I offered. I was really sorry that she wasn't doing! So later in the evening I put on my wellies and my boiler suit and went with Daddy to the cow. She was just about to collapse. "We'd better bring her down to the shed," urged Daddy.

We were thumping and pushing and kicking. Eventually we got her to the shed. In the pen she collapsed. We tried to give her some nuts but she refused them. It was looking bad. Eventually Daddy rang the vet who came and gave her a dose of magnesium. "Better get her warm in her pen," said the vet as he left.

We got a rope and tried to pull her out. We slid her across the floor and when we came to a bump we had to rest. After a while we gave the rope a big tug and the cow got over.

With a bed of straw and an old blanket we made her comfortable. She refused to drink. After a while we came and checked the cow again. In the morning the vet came and gave her more magnesium, and in the evening she was standing.

I could see the relief on Daddy's face.

"It's great stuff, that magnesium," he said. "She's going to do."

And so she did.

Neal Coll
Pupil

"Let some sunlight in ..."

Summer Night Haiku

Breathe that soft night air
Honeysuckle-scented mist
Summer's new-mown hay.

Margaret Boucher
Teacher

"I chase ideas as if they were butterflies..."

Taking Flight

I find it hard to put into words how much I enjoyed and benefited from my week in Baronscourt. I was astounded by the inspired pieces of writing which the children produced in the log cabin; the uninhibited expression of their experience through sculpture and their willingness to offer their art back as a gift to the earth; how freely the children took on the essence of their chosen feature of the environment in the drama workshop; the beautiful musical performances; and the dedication of all the children to work with their fellow team members in the Baronscourt challenge. Most of all, I thoroughly enjoyed being a participant in all the activities.

In Froebel College we have been learning the importance of providing an environment in which children can learn through discovery, while avoiding the use of unnecessary boundaries and negative criticism. During the week of the Baronscourt Summer Camp of the Imagination I saw this theory take flight, as I watched each child blossom.

Mairéad Ennis
Student Teacher, 2003

"...the opportunity to share, to explore and to grow..."

The Power of Pushkin

I have worked for Pushkin since the first Summer Camp of the Imagination in 1998. But I would not really call it working. I would call it enjoying myself or having a good time! I have facilitated at all of the Summer Camps and each year on the Baronscourt Days and I was also involved in the Partners in Education programme, with trainee teachers and their lecturers in Glenstal Abbey. My role is that of an environmental facilitator but as Head Gardener in Baronscourt I help out with whatever needs to be done when it comes to Pushkin events.

When I take groups of children and adults out for an environmental workshop I generally work in the woodland garden and in the formal garden. The approach I take is just free and easy. Whatever happens happens! I try to guide the children in certain areas and allow them to ask their own questions so that really they decide what shape the workshop takes. We look at different varieties of trees and talk about how trees from vastly different countries, like the Tibetan cherry, can survive in this climate too. We look for interesting bugs and smells and we work out why certain plants have a nice smell and others have a pungent smell. We use all our senses but we don't taste things. We focus a lot on the 'feel' of things, like the feel of the roots of the ash tree through the soles of our footwear (mainly wellies for obvious reasons!)

I find the mix of adults and children in the groups works very well. I see them all as equals and it is always great to see how amazed the teachers are by what they are discovering about the environment. They are also often amazed by what the children already know. There is nothing as nice as seeing a child stand up to tell all they know to the rest of the group, to see that spark of imagination and the way their eyes light up. It is very gratifying. I enjoy showing and telling children what they may not have seen or heard before. I find it a very humbling experience to be in the position of passing on some information and of having that information so graciously received by the adults and children. It always amazes me when it comes to the writing workshops in the log cabin. The children who say they can't write are usually the ones that you can't get stopped once they start! Some of the stories and poems that they write can be very moving. Somehow the Summer Camp week or even a Baronscourt day can touch them very deeply.

Great credit is due to the Duchess for bringing Pushkin to life, for making all of this happen. She has contributed so much and given so freely of her time and energies over the years. No honour she could receive for everything she has done would be great enough.

Being involved in Pushkin has changed me. It has softened my approach and outlook on the world. And Pushkin has been very important in developing relationships both north and south of the border and across the religious and political divides. Through its work with the environment children have learned that they have a role in looking after things, that what they do is important and that their voices do count.

Larry Monteith
Environmental Facilitator

In the Beginning

The year was 1987 and I had been seconded from my teaching post to the Western Education and Library Board as a Field Officer, working with schools in the implementation of the recently published Primary Guidelines for Language and Literacy. I recall the afternoon I received a phone call summoning me back to headquarters to meet with the Chief Executive, Mr Murphy, and his visitor, the Duchess of Abercorn.

Her greeting was warm and friendly and right away, I sensed a kindred spirit. "You are involved in working on Literacy," said Mr. Murphy. "Her Grace has a wonderful idea that I'd like you to help her take forward." No pressure, then!

I listened carefully as Her Grace outlined the purpose of her visit. Our school system was largely segregated. 'Troubles' were a way of life and children were being educated against a background of conflict. The Duchess was a mother and her daughter was being visited by nightmares and bad dreams and she was no longer prepared to be a passive observer. She was also the great, great, great granddaughter of the Russian poet, Alexander Pushkin who as a boy loved to listen to Russian tales narrated by his old nanny. Inspired by this, the Duchess wanted to channel the imagination and energies of our children into the world of fairytales and folklore, of heart and hearth. They would find kindred spirits and new role models across the divide. They would form friendships and create a new story for their time. And so, seeds were sown that day that would germinate in hearts and minds, put down secure roots, sprout many branches, and grow strong and tall over the next twenty-five years and beyond.

It was decided in the first year that eight schools would be chosen, four from the Western Board and four from Donegal. The schools were to be paired across the

border and across the religious divide and children would create a new fairytale to be read and enjoyed by children in their partner schools. There were also inter-school visits arranged and Her Grace would visit each of the schools during the year with a grand celebration in Baronscourt to culminate the year the following June.

This in 1987 was ground breaking stuff and it would never have taken off without the support of the Western Board and Harry Cheevers, a school inspector in Donegal, who identified schools for participation and later would sell the idea to the Department of Education in the Republic of Ireland.

Some years later, reflecting on the reasons for its success, Michael Murphy summed it up under the heading 'enthusiasm.' Firstly, he said there was the enthusiasm of the children of Ireland for their writing. Secondly, there was the enthusiasm of the participating schools and teachers who stimulated the children and encouraged them to see themselves in the slipstream of great writers from Ireland and beyond. Then there was the enthusiasm of the Departments of Education, North and South and the Education and Library Boards which had supported the project from its inception and welcomed its contribution to the creative, cultural, social and intellectual development of all the participants. Finally and most importantly, he said, there was the enthusiasm of The Duchess of Abercorn, who through her history and background had brought vision, sensitivity and inspiration to the Pushkin Prizes.

It is the Duchess' enthusiasm that is key to why, after a quarter of a century, we are still celebrating Pushkin when so many so-called 'initiatives' in education have fizzled and died in that time. The essential ingredient, the magic mix that makes this so enduring is the breadth of vision of the Duchess and her continuing involvement. She has held fast to that vision for twenty-five years. She has articulated it, developed, facilitated and nurtured it and all the while she has allowed it to take its own momentum, branch out and diverge, while holding firmly to that inner ground, the strong central core of her beliefs.

It has been a privilege to share in that experience and to have been part of this story from the beginning. I take great heart in the realisation that the Pushkin story is still unfolding, into its twenty-sixth year. I look forward to seeing the new shoots of growth that will emerge in the years ahead, secure in the knowledge that the Pushkin tap root runs deep.

Shiela McCaul
Pushkin Trustee

My Leafy Protector

Butterflies land on
buttercups,
like door-to-door
salesmen.
Foxes peer outside
their dens,
as if seeing the
world for the
first time.

Hares box in the
long-grassed fields,
and lambs frolic
and dance.
The mare and the foal
gallop and graze
in the pastureland
beside me.
All these things I
overlook from my
hut in the trees.

Peter McGettigan
Pupil

"My heart burst open and all my dreams fell on the page..."

Letting Creativity Flow

Pushkin was one of the most rewarding projects in which I was involved over my teaching career. The number of children who benefited from the various programmes is considerable, particularly children for whom the academic end of the curriculum was a challenge. The confidence and enhanced self-esteem of some of these children was matched only by their incredible standard of creativity.

I remember the year the Pushkin theme was *The River of Life*. I was teaching in a mixed sixth class in the North Dublin National School Project in Glasnevin. We had spoken at length about our personal rivers of life and I had had asked the children to write a passage about their own life's journey. Walking around the room monitoring progress, I noticed one boy doodling on a page rather than writing. As he was a particularly creative and artistic boy, I said nothing and waited. The result was amazing. Rather than write a piece of text, he had chosen to draw an illustrated version of his river as it passed through the various phases of his life to date, with sharp bends, forks and long straight stretches. The miniature images he drew along the way were perfect. The other children were so taken with his interpretation of the assignment that they abandoned their own work and they too drew their own 'Rivers of Life.' It was such a wonderful example of a child's imagination being given free rein.

Alice Ring
Pushkin Regional Leader, 2006-2007

"Children are worth listening to...."

My Dad

My dad is a
tickle-monster
night-tucker-inner
game-wizard
my healer
cuddle-monster
homework-helper.
My dad,
dish-washer
breakfast-machine
heart-curer
decision-helper.
That's why I love my dad so much!

Nicola Fyffe
Pupil

"Imagination is one of the few things that cannot be taken away from you and expressing it on paper is a wonderful talent to have."

The Art of the Pushkin Dance

My first encounter with the Pushkin programme revealed a creative ethos and vision that was transforming and sustaining. From the outset there was a sense of permission to create and to be creative through the Pushkin experience in my facilitation. I sensed that this permission gave teachers, children and facilitating artists a critically expressive space through which to explore and open new creative ways to knowledge and being.

The excitement for me is always in that moment when the door of the classroom opens or the dark green door of the Pushkin conference space opens and the children flood in to begin their exploration of creative dance and expression of the Pushkin theme of that year. At times, on entering the space, their little bodies and sense of themselves can be withdrawn and anxious and the challenge is to provide a safe dance pathway through which they can release and express the many textures of their young beings. The critical self-expression accessed through learning the skills of contemporary dance offers the children a new creative language that builds confidence, knowledge and achievement.

When I reflect on key Pushkin moments, my mind is transported to the many perceived less-able children who have and continue to enter into the 'Pushkin education space.' I recollect in particular one little, excited boy who was quite frightened and was described as "very disruptive." I was advised that he needed his teaching assistant by his side at all times. His lack of self-confidence and self-esteem were palpable. However from the outset of the warm-up exercise where the children offered a movement that expressed who they were, I could see a glimpse of this young child's ability to access his creativity more easily than the other children in the workshop. He excelled from the beginning of the class and was by far the most creatively-gifted and focussed child in the group despite his label of being "very disruptive."

I remember that day being really amazed at how much this lively boy contributed to that workshop and how he roguishly, but sensitively, worked alongside the other children to express the meaning of 'connecting.' He stretched out lively arms and legs to connect across the space, linking with some of the children from the other participating school as well as those in his class. Throughout the workshop he contributed positively and integrated with the other children. At times he directed the movement patterns in his group. I was thrilled but not surprised when his teaching assistant commented;

"I can't believe he is so focussed and engaged. He is like a different boy. I am so thrilled to see him accepted by the other children. Just imagine what he would be like if he had this every day. By the way, I am having great fun too!"

The experience and outcome of this child's Baronscourt Day workshop has been the experience and story of many of the perceived less-able children who have had the opportunity to access and achieve new levels through the unique Pushkin programme. The unlocking of their creativity and that of their teachers in a safe, ethical, creative space has offered both the teacher and the child an opportunity to flourish and enhance not only the education experience but the critical teacher-pupil relationship, bringing a fresh, shared, creative vision into the classroom.

As a dance artist and facilitator, the Pushkin Trust experience has given me an opportunity to flourish within my craft and personal creativity through the support of the Pushkin Trust's committed founder, The Duchess of Abercorn, the Pushkin staff and the other Pushkin arts and environmental facilitators.

On reflection, the Pushkin programme is the critical breath of education and creativity.

Jenny Elliott
Contemporary Dance Facilitator

Vivid Childhood Memories

As a Primary 7 pupil I had the opportunity to take part in the Pushkin Summer Camp of the Imagination. As a very timid eleven year old I didn't know what to expect but from the very moment I arrived in Baronscourt I felt such a sense of welcoming. There were children from all over Ireland playing together, having fun together, making lasting friendships and most importantly they were learning together.

From nature walks with Lynn and garden walks with Larry to music with Elaine and dance with Steve and not forgetting writing workshops with Joan, Kate and their dog Beau in the log cabin. The vibrant grounds filled with wild flowers, herbs and bright colours, the labyrinth that I could spend hours in, the sheer enormity and grandeur of Baronscourt, especially 'the big house.' I recall so many memorable moments. Through the many workshops provided by the Summer Camp, I have grown as an individual and I have taken the skills that I have learnt and utilised them, not just throughout my school years but in my life as a whole. The pinnacle of my Pushkin journey has got to be winning the Pushkin Prize in 2000. I still have a copy of my portfolio that was judged to be the all-Ireland winner. I use it as my claim to fame – even putting it on my CV! Getting to spend prize day in Baronscourt in the presence of The Duchess of Abercorn and many famous writers is still a vivid memory from my childhood.

Gráinne O'Kane
Teacher

*"The Pushkin project made me realise
that there is no limit to how creative and imaginative
the human mind can be..."*

Winter's Wrath

The sky darkens
Clouds call forth their families
Casting dark shadows around
Mean and evil they spread
Their shrouds
An ominous sign!
Droplets of rain, tiny at first
Tap our heads and window panes.
Slowly, slowly puddles shape
Then a deluge
Sweeps across our towns and lands
Helped by an angry wind
At first a whisper, then a roar
What will quench his craving thirst?

In the woodland, trees succumb
Breaking branches, hopes are dashed
As giant trees by roots are slashed
Years of effort strewn about.
In towns, an eerie sound
    Doors slam
    Gates crash
    Boxes roll
    Bins topple
    Bottles smash
What an anger winter's unleashed.

Up and down the streets
Leaves and rubbish zip along
Dancing amidst this angry throng.
Alone, a cyclist fighting back
Holding hard against attack
Footsteps trudge close to walls
Brollies, hats fight off the squall
As the storm hunts its prey.
Mercilessly it reaches out
It shrieking fangs
To grab and crush
All in its way.

Birds fly low to their homes
To find shelter from this foe
Animals cower in their shed
Not too sure what it is they dread
Buildings standing, start to sway
Soon demolished on the way
Out at sea, boats rock and roll
Foam spits and frolics against the bay
Throughout the night storms
Echo and growl
An angry lion on its prowl
At first light silence abounds
Birds were all that made their sounds
What damage lay for us today?
"Storms Lashed"
The papers say.

Anna Murray
Pupil

Pushkin ... Building Smashing Towers

Some months ago on a Baronscourt day, as a happy contingent of youngsters trooped their way from the stableyard to the Log Cabin between the two lakes, one young man looked in astonishment at Barons Court and exclaimed: "God, that's a quare size of a B&B, sir!" To be addressed as Sir some hundred yards from where Their Graces abide must count as a seminal moment in what has been a gloriously creative and fun-filled odyssey in the past two decades as a Pushkin facilitator. Whatever about the magic that happens within the cabin, the journeys there have always had their own fascination. Some three or four years ago on a beautiful Spring day, 'Jimmy', a child with Asperger's syndrome, literally took over the role of creative writing facilitator, and on the way back to the Log Cabin after lunch (he had insisted on two sessions!) stuck to his morning imaginative exercises while his fellow pupils danced and bounced along after a slight increase in their sugar content.

We had been working on 'word associations' and Jimmy looked with fascination at the array of young lambs on the hill below the stables. "Stop!" he shouted, at which command he pointed up at the woolly snowflakes dotted along the horizon. Then he turned to me and said with great satisfaction: "Mint Sauce!"

Frank Galligan
Poet

"Pushkin opened a new door for me. Usually my dyslexia closes doors."

Amazing Roots

These roots are wild and fearsome
like a mad dog hunting for its prey.
They struggle and squirm
along the forest floor.
Their roots slither and slide
like a python snake slinking underground.
The suction of their octopus tentacles
holds the tree
sternly to the ground.
These roots are comfortable homes
for animals and minibeasts.
Here hedgehogs hibernate,
foxes, badgers and cubs.
Worms wriggle,
beetles giggle,
What a wonderful
Underground world!

Mark Gallagher
Pupil

"The thrill of sharing our words with others...."

Drowning in the Imagination

I come from the land of the eleven plus (a horrible experience of unnatural selection through so-called intelligence tests.) Most of my latter school days were spent preparing for those fateful sixty minutes of terror, and so if it were not for the Pushkin Prize, my life may have been very different.

Her Grace, The Duchess of Abercorn came to my school in 1987 and spoke to us about her ancestor, Alexander Pushkin and his love of words. We heard about her idea for the prize, how anyone could enter and that we could write absolutely anything. She went on to reveal that there would be no points given or deducted on the basis of grammar or spelling. I was in! She talked about how we were future authors from a country where the imagination was alive and well. I think that one of the most beautiful things about the whole concept of the Pushkin Prize is that in a land where borders and walls cause so many problems, we were given a chance to break them all down. Go anywhere, say anything, be anyone. The vehicle we would use to take us there was our imagination.

I often wonder why children paint the sky as a blue line across the top of the page. Perhaps that's just how they see it. In a child's mind the world is a different place. We can learn a lot from that place, but all too often we fly through those years and leave no record of what it was like. We grow up. I had a strange floating feeling when I wrote as a child and I look for it all the time now. The feeling of drowning in my imagination. I have to remind myself I was smaller then, small enough to believe whatever I wanted to.

I write almost everyday now. It is a little different from writing for the Pushkin Prize as an eleven year old. I have no memory of criticism back then, but now when I go away to write I often fight off demons in the back of my head. They tell me to tread carefully over minefields of clichés and to hide my naivety under a cloak of experience that I may not have. More and more I am trying to relearn that valuable lesson given to me by the Pushkin Prize. There are no rules. I love the feeling of knowing that.

I can't say what I would be doing today had I not entered the Pushkin Prize. I know it has affected me greatly. For the first time I realised that people might be interested in what I had to say. I do know that when her Grace came to that room and to many others like it since, we were shown an open door. The door would lead anywhere we wanted.

John McDaid
First Pushkin prizewinner and singer-songwriter in *Snow Patrol*

John Moriarty Thinks of Pushkin and the Children of Ireland

Over twenty years ago I came to Pushkin with my crane bag of words. I met children, teachers and student teachers in schools and colleges, hotels with hushed corridors and fabulous food; one time, a room in the Hugh Lane with Clarke's *Eve of St. Agnes* glittering blue. Mostly I went to Baronscourt. My first visit I was awed by the clock tower and courtyard, unaware that the much grander house was down the road.

"The mortgage must be *huge*," said a little girl with an old head, as we trooped past on our way to the Log Cabin where the writing groups go. I'd light a fire in the stove and leave the door open to a field of daffodils.

From the very beginning I had to teach grammar, because it has 'grown out of fashion like an old song.' Postcards helped us find nouns, verbs, adjectives and adverbs. Lists of words. The building blocks of literature. They closed their eyes as I led them through an imaginary forest and into a clearing. *Write what you saw there.* Such crowded, noisy imaginations – castles, hunting hounds, a fire-breathing dragon, ancient battles, dancing bears, fairies. Those were the years when I paraded the sestina, a template for epic poems. We were all delighted with ourselves!

Then came the time when I saw that a sestina was too much to ask. I opened my crane bag and found acrostics for poems, comic strips and posters for prose. There was a lack of vocabulary, an impoverished literacy, but when I led them to the clearing, they still saw castles, armies, dragons and fairies. But here is something you need to know. These past few years, they can barely write a sentence. And worse than that, the dark despairing thing: when I bring them through the forest and into the glade, more and more of the children say they see … nothing.

One day, a single class came into the Log Cabin. A single class came in and they wrote such poems and stories and they said, "don't bother with acrostics we do them all the time show us something new." It was because of her. Their teacher. "I love literature," she said. "I love books. I love words." She had her own crane bag and all year long she had opened it so that when her children came to me they could sing like the children of Lir in full flight.

Some years ago, I went to a teacher's college for their Pushkin day. A writer, a poet, a musician and an artist, we all arrived with our crane bags. The day was optional, their free choice, and not a single student teacher came. Not one. Perhaps they needed to rest, perhaps they needed to study for their exams; but if only someone had told them that they need to have a crane bag when they go to teach the children. They need the crane bag of words or the crane bag of art or the crane bag of music when they go to teach the children. Because if they do not open the crane bag for the children, the children will go through the Great Forest and they will see nothing. The children will see nothing.

The children will see nothing.

OR Melling
Writer, screenwriter and literary critic

Opening Windows of Wonder

The 18th February 1998 is still a stand-out day in the history of St.Teresa's N.S., Killoe, in County Longford. That was the day that Her Grace, The Duchess of Abercorn first visited our school. The day dawned crisp and bright and an air of expectation hung over the school. This marked the culmination of a month's hard work as staff, pupils and the school community busily prepared to receive our special guest. When the moment of the Duchess' arrival came all the pent-up tension was immediately dissipated by her warm smile and easy manner. The children immediately responded to her presence and gave her a resounding Killoe welcome through their poems, stories, music, song and dance.

The visit coincided with the death of a great teacher and writer Bryan McMahon. He, through his teaching and writing, had endeavoured to "open windows of wonder" for the children to ignite their creative talents. The Duchess' mantra has always been to sow seeds of creativity through the use of the imagination, and in so doing, to help children to find a voice for their creative instincts. When reflecting on his contribution to education the similarity between his approach and the ethos of Pushkin is striking.

The title for that year's creative writing was *The Giant at my Shoulder*. Those children who took part in 1998 are now adults and they still speak in glowing terms of the Duchess' keen interest in their work and of her inspirational presence on that day. From a school perspective, hosting such an occasion offered all an opportunity to come together in a spirit of co-operation, to welcome our guest and affirm the children's efforts. This partnership approach allowed us all to grow and sowed the seeds of co-operation that have served us well since that time. The special experience of the first visit injected the impetus in all of us to remain connected. We are very pleased that the school is still engaged in the Pushkin initiative some fifteen years later. We are fortunate to still have the influence of the 'giant at our shoulder' gently nudging us forward and affirming all our efforts.

We are particularly proud of the fact that the seeds of creativity sown in that first visit have yielded a rich harvest and a number of the 'crop' of 1998 has continued to find a voice for their creative abilities. In fact a number of those pupils have had their creative efforts published and acclaimed at national level. At the moment we are busily engaged in ploughing new furrows and look forward to sharing the fruits of our labour with The Duchess of Abercorn on her next visit.

Colm Harte
Teacher and Pushkin Regional Leader, 2003-2007

"... I believe its enduring value is in carving new songlines of perception ..."

The Inestimable Value of Creative Writing

Pushkin Prizes Trust, established by Sacha, The Duchess of Abercorn in 1987, has facilitated writers to visit schools and confirm the inestimable value of creative writing with teachers and pupils. It was a remarkable and beneficial gift to be given to Ireland and I am honoured, having been invited by Ann McKay, to have been part of it.

Recently I found notes I had made years ago on creating a place for creative writing, and I still believe this:

> *Childhood is the state of grace from which we fall. What right have adults to tell children that the adult world with its duplicity, its shabbiness, its greed, its unhappiness, is what has to be reached for.*

> *Perhaps there are no words for the complexity of what we are feeling or recollecting and we have to use what there are in the only way we know. This may not comply with the rules of grammar but the rules of grammar must bend when something new and fresh and vital is being born into words.*

> *It's not a teaching situation. You cannot give your student anything except the knowledge that there is no room for censure, half-truths or sneering: that the ethos is one of support and encouragement and admiration. And you are in it as well. You have to give yourself and often your attempts, which might be guarded or self-conscious or complacent and may not be as good in terms of the quality of creative writing as the most illiterate child. You need to acknowledge this to yourself, even better, publicly. Everyone else will already know.*

> *It is not work you should attempt unless you are fully alive and generous and love the magic of the word wherever it is found.*

> *It isn't teaching. It is complete participation by everyone and by it we learn each other.*

I made over five hundred visits to schools. What was said has lived with me, especially a piece by Eilish McLoughlin in a school in Edgeworthstown. Her first memory (and I quote from the original):

> *My first real memory was when my father died. I was brushing my hair to go to tennis practice. I seen daddy's leg on the ground and thought he was messing because mammy screamed. I went into the room and he was on the ground. He wasn't moving. We went into my granny's side and called an ambulance. Lots of people came over and I realised daddy was dead.*

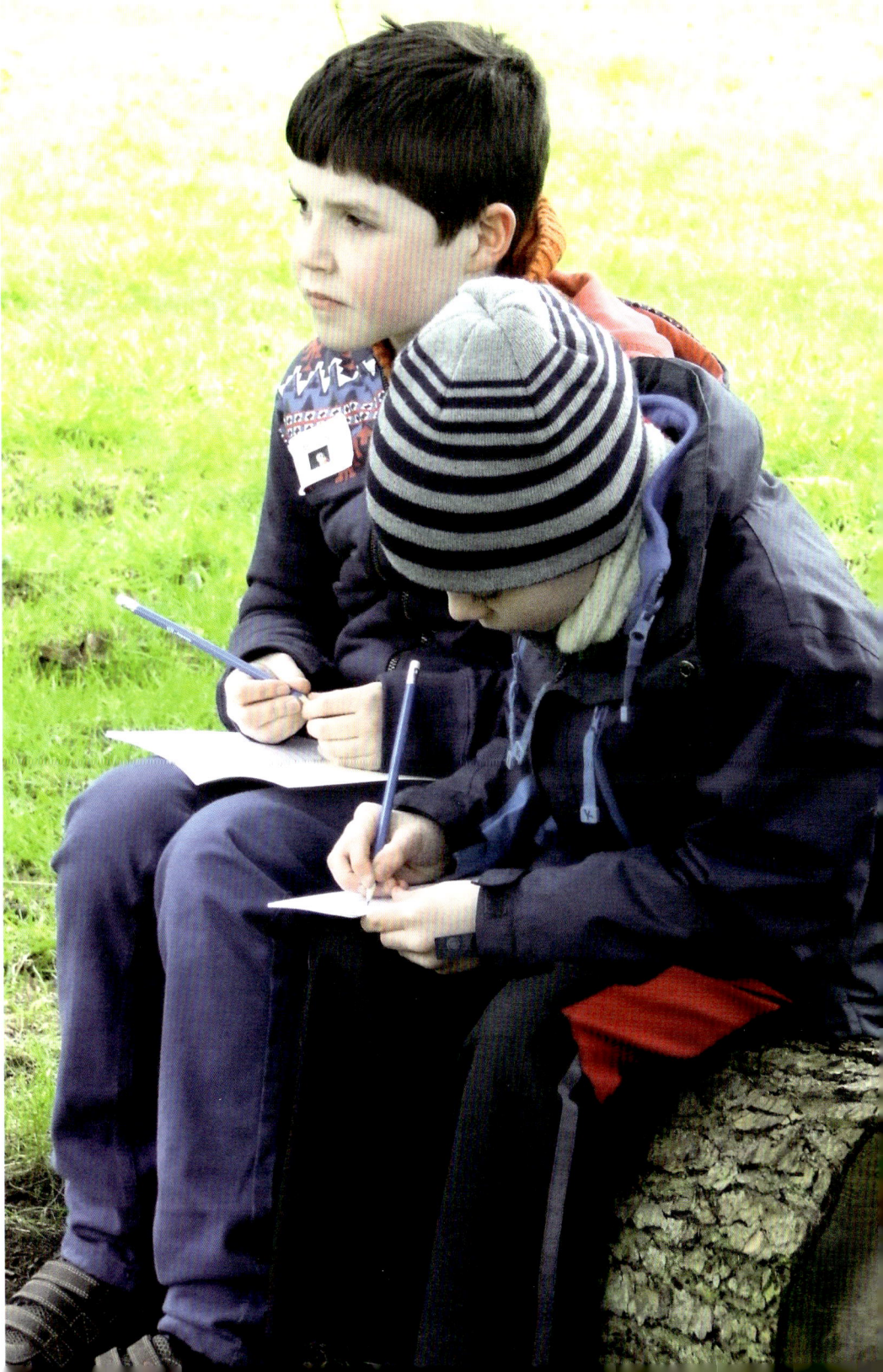

When Eilish had finished reading there was absolute silence in the classroom. After a pause I thanked Eilish for having given me something I will never forget. It is strange to think that she is in her twenties. I sincerely hope that her amazing courage and vision and honesty and clarity and a knowledge, that to say herself, is her right – has remained with her. Both of us, on that day, were grateful to Pushkin.

Joan Newmann
Poet

Hippo

A lazy flopper.
A slow runner,
A foot-plodder,
A territory-hogger,
A grey blob,
A water-swimmer,
A leg-breaker,
A veggy eater.

Ronan Geraghty
Pupil

*"I learned to let my mind wander
and imagine things with my senses."*

Excavating the Crevices of Memory

Back in 2005 I had the pleasure of facilitating poetry workshops at Annaghmakerrig in July, and later at Glenstal Abbey in the Fall for the Pushkin Trust, for teachers and trainee teachers respectively. Given the spectacular setting of each location it is not surprising the arresting creativity that flowed from the participants.

What has remained in the crevices of memory is, how the world looked after rain on the lawn in Annaghmakerrig, the shadows darkness offered up to the lake before swimming, and of how, a coldness pervaded towards dawn in Lady Guthrie's bedroom, during the week of the 7/7 London bombings.

Also what springs to mind is disturbing the dew on early morning walks through the forest at Glenstal. And of Paddy Madden introducing me to Hart's Tongue as robins guided us past uprooted rhododendron on the path to the Mass Rock. And of course, the mesmeric choreography of Gregorian chant that still echoes like rubato.

Something intangible happened in the dynamic of those present on both occasions. In a free-flowing of imaginations, creativity became unbound and friendships forged, giving a sense of meaning and place that may have been previously displaced.

Mass Rock at Glenstal

As I place my hands on the altar, a tingling slows
the contours of my fingertips, wells-up its topography
like an Ordnance Survey Sheet; number in relief,
or when ink from an immigration pad at Shannon left
a Hart's Tongue-print like the fern before me all over
this blessed flock wallpaper of ours; where I've traced
and retraced times spent listening to family histories,
the Rising, price of the pint and good weather for drying.

Anne Fitzgerald
Poet

Pushkin's Gift to the Children of Ireland

It was my privilege to work with Pushkin from 2000 until 2010, firstly as a teacher and subsequently as the Trust's Development Director for five years. I use the word 'privilege' because my discovery of all things Pushkin was not just an opportunity but it became a professionally rewarding and personally life-enhancing journey. It was a perfect way to round off my career in education and I look back on those years with deep affection and satisfaction.

I watched the children in my classes respond eagerly, expressing themselves from the heart through creative writing, poetry and cross-curricular project work. These activities took on a life of their own, inspired by the children's sense of purpose, freed from the more rigid conventions associated with spelling, grammar and handwriting.

Not of course, that these were jettisoned but they were 'suspended' temporarily whilst time was given to freeing the imagination and allowing minds to dream without hindrance. The results raised self-esteem, often markedly so for those children who were not necessarily high-flyers or who were simply reserved and shy. So too, more gifted children explored their capabilities with evident relish.

My time as Director afforded me some wonderful opportunities to meet educators, to travel to parts of Ireland new to me and most important of all, to see the amazing work done in schools by dedicated and inspiring teachers. Whilst it is clear to me that Pushkin has achieved significant and effective links with Colleges of Education and teachers around Ireland, it is this work with children that has most directly impacted on the nurturing of creativity and has facilitated mutual understanding in both parts of our island.

All of us who have been in any way involved in the work of the Pushkin Trust are truly grateful to Sacha for her vision, inspirational leadership and her determination to give young people here in Ireland a voice. And so, the deeply personal words, music, art and dance created by so many children over the last twenty-five successful years, will forever be the true spirit of Pushkin in a land now beginning to sense real healing.

Alan Boyd
Former Development Director with the Pushkin Trust

The Bog Song

Johnny Nora made the spade
sing in the bog
vibrating against the upturned sod
as the notes hung in the June air,
reverberating on stones and heather.
Were I to see him now,
his foot would be heavy, his digging slow.
the tune this time chipped and low.

I know there will come a time
when there will be no songs left to sing.
In the November chill the spade will lie
in the bog
that history will have painted with flightless doves.
And I, perhaps too far out to reach,
like a fallen star washed up on a beach,
will hear this melody knock against my bones,
in place of heather and busted stones.

Susan Doherty
Teacher

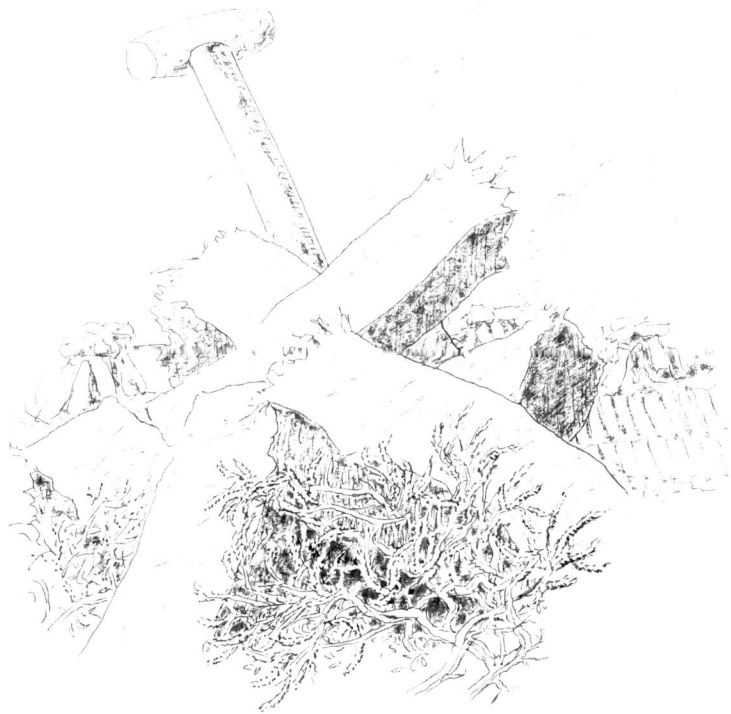

"*I come from a fairytale that's never been told ...*"

The Pushkin Grail Quest

Imagination is the bright, illuminating flame of a life richly lived, and teachers who wish to nourish the imaginations of the young people in their charge have to take care that their own imaginations are kept well alight. The Pushkin Trust has always worked hard to help them in this essential aspect of their work, and a few years ago I was lucky enough to be invited as a teacher of creative writing to take part in a Partners-In-Education week designed to bring a group of trainee teachers from all parts of Ireland together at Baronscourt in order to foster their creativity.

In searching for a theme which would hold the group together while allowing plenty of scope for individuals to express themselves imaginatively, it occurred to me that inspiration might be drawn from an old story which has long been dear to my heart – the story of Parzival's quest for the Grail. At first sight this might seem an odd choice. After all what bearing could a medieval legend about knights and ladies have on the priorities of young teachers about to accept responsibility for educating children into the complexities of life in a new millennium? The answer lies in the way the tale addresses what James Joyce once called the grave and constant themes of the human heart.

Like all of us, Parzival is born in ignorance of the world. After his father's violent death, his mother, desperate to protect her son from the same fate, withdraws with him into the wilderness. He grows up as an innocent fool, untutored in the ways of the world until a vision of fame and glory – the desire to become one of King Arthur's knights – draws him out in search of his destiny. At Arthur's court the complexities of the world quickly close round him. Mocked as a bumpkin, he resolves to prove himself a true knight but is soon led into difficulties by unquestioning obedience to authority and by his own stubborn will. Eventually, a series of disasters, including news of the death of his mother, reduce his life to a quest for meaning in a wasteland time.

Much of what happens to Parzival closely corresponds to each of us as we attempt to understand an adult world fraught with difficulties and conflict, while trying to find an authentic place for ourselves inside it. Parzival comes to learn that the truth of one's inner conscience can be a surer guide to right action than obedience to even well-meaning mentors. He also discovers that a mature integrity can be the reward of undergoing ordeals of the heart, while the unfolding theme of the story insists that something new is made for life only through reconciliation of opposing elements. Above all, it affirms the power of compassion as a healing force.

Participants in the course were encouraged to listen for motifs in the story which resonated with important aspects of their own experience, and then to write out of that confluence. The deeply affecting results gave ample evidence that the young teachers of Ireland are rich in creative resources, and that the Pushkin Trust continues to work well in fostering the power of imagination as an agent of change and reconciliation in these transitional times.

Lindsay Clarke
Writer

The Beach

The waves under my feet.
The old lighthouse on the hill,
rusted and red.
Soft sand between my toes.
Children with their buckets and
spades having fun
in the cool sea breeze.
The faraway coastline in the
horizon,
wonder where it is …
A rugged mass of rocks, under which people sit
and watch the sea.
The ice-cream man with his cold chilly ice-creams …
Rows of cars and more cars,
Rows of people higgly-piggly on the beach.
The siren sounds from the amusements
and the crashing of the bumper cars.
The ageless fortune teller with her multicoloured hut,
spinning stories for silver.
Happy children on donkeys, going round and round the beach …
Shops selling ornaments which state "Ireland,"
restaurants bursting at the seams,
coach-loads of Americans booking into hotels.
The smell of the sun-lotion and chips.

People standing at the water's edge,

they're walking their dogs.

Kids flying their kites, far up to the sky.

People queue to look through the telescope for 20p.

Children on the swings and slides,

loving every minute.

People panting and puffing after a long walk.

An occasional speed-boat whizzes past,

Leaving a white surf behind.

Crabs, jelly fish and weeds on the beach.

The smell of a nearby barbecue and the sound of sizzling sausages.

The cry of a kid who has lost his Mum.

The smack of a tennis ball against the racquet.

The tide begins to come in.

The day is almost over.

People pack up belongings and get ready for home.

The ringing of a winning jackpot bell –

someone is happy

A last look around on a quiet beach.

It is quiet, empty and somehow colder.

I shiver and off I go

home.

Gerard Connolly
Pupil

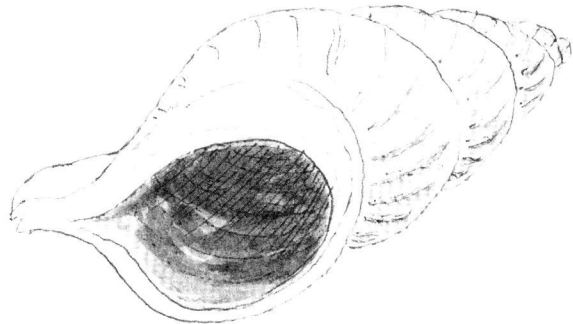

Dear Aisling

You wrote to ask me a question. Why Pushkin? Your school is thinking of getting involved with Pushkin. So why Pushkin? My simple answer is – why not? You've been teaching now for three years. I look back fifty years to when I was at that stage of my career. I cringe more than a little. Earnest, uncertain, wary. At training college my classroom mentor had written of my "stern and stilted attitude ... he must 'loosen up' and present a less funereal countenance to the children." Ah me, if only I had Pushkin then!

You work in a system that is obsessed with measurement and accountability. Fight it! Remember the words of the great 'measuring man', Albert Einstein – "Not everything that is countable counts – and not everything that counts, is countable." The happiest days of my teaching career were the days that I stepped off the treadmill and did something that was not necessarily "countable." When you take on a Pushkin project, you and your pupils will drink from that refreshing well of possibility that it offers. You will experience the great sense of release that Michelangelo spoke of when he "saw" the statue in the block of marble and continued to chip away until the figure emerged. That is **your** calling as a teacher – to chip away at all that is not the child and ultimately free that child to be itself and find its true voice. It won't always be easy. It will take courage, but it will be rewarding. The uncertain path is always ultimately more liberating.

You are well named, Aisling. Your name means the dream, the vision. Follow that vision with your pupils. In the words of Seamus Heaney (a patron of Pushkin!)

> *Let go, let fly, forget,*
> *You've listened long enough,*
> *Now strike your note,*

That is what the creative art is all about – striking **your** note, exploring **your** possibility – mindful of Emily Dickinson's words –

> *I dwell in possibility*
> *A fairer house than prose*
> *Superior for windows*
> *More numerous of doors.*

Throw open those windows, Aisling. Go and open the Pushkin door. You and your teaching will never be the same again.

Best wishes,
John Quinn
Writer and Pushkin Trustee

'The Pushkin Species'

I remember one particular environmental walk around the Baronscourt grounds with Lynn. She handed each child a piece of coloured wool and asked them to toss it into the bushes. It was very easy to retrieve them. Next she asked them to throw in strands of green-coloured wool. These, of course, were harder to find and so a salutary lesson on predators and camouflage was taught. I have often used this experiment with my classes in the intervening years to great effect.

However, I always had a niggling thought in my mind that this concept of Nature didn't follow through in the context of the Pushkin experience. Let me explain.

When you went to Baronscourt (or the Tyrone Guthrie Centre, in Annaghmakerrig) you entered a different world. You started off as that little piece of green wool; eager to participate, to become one of a special group, to savour the whole sense of community and security in a common literary objective. Yet as the week progressed, you became one of those brightly-coloured strands; finding your own voice and spirit – while buttressed by the genuine warmth and enthusiasm of all around you. Did you feel vulnerable, about to be devoured by predatory forces? No, you felt liberated and inspired, ready to take on the world!

So, Lynn, there is another classification that defies definition; a species that blends into the background and yet stands out as unique and creative, without fear of submission. Only those who have experienced the 'essence' of the Pushkin journey can truly understand my point of view.

Valerie Murphy
Teacher

*"Listen to the silence of this other world
and you too can become part of its magic."*

Pushkin Magic

During one Summer Camp of the Imagination, many years ago, Bill, the musician, taught the children a catchy warm-up song about flowers and sunshine at the beginning of all his workshops. None of us could get it out of our heads!

At the end of the week during the Baronscourt Challenge evening I was sitting in the middle of the forest propped up against a pine tree near the Ski Hut. I was hiding and waiting to award bonus points to the participating teams of children, teachers and facilitators for good team work, staying safely together in groups, being happy, brilliant singing – (and for giving bars of chocolate to environmentalists!) – as they made their way around the estate in search of The Challenge clues.

I was enjoying a precious few moments of peace and quiet in a hectic week. Evening sunbeams were casting long-angled shadows through the woodland. Insects were dancing in the sunshine and there wasn't a breath of wind. A warm tranquil evening – a perfect world.

Gradually I became aware of the distant echo of children's voices singing Bill's wonderful song all around the forest. I shut my eyes and listened. It was almost surreal. It was truly magical. Pushkin magic.

Jess Webb
Environmentalist

"... making the ordinary, extraordinary ..."

Thoughts of a Snowdrop Bulb

I am pressurising soil
where I was born.
The soil smells fresh
just like Fabreeze.

I feel roots,
other snowdrops,
gravity,
air.
I exit to shoot out.

I feel people standing on me.
I'm being watered by thumping rain
And the worms are still teasing me.

Emma Ward
Pupil

Alongside evening song-singing, music-playing, story-telling and dancing, we marvel at the talent among our future teachers and at the cultural diversity across the island of Ireland. It reinforces how important the creative arts are in education as a means of embracing diversity and cross cultural co-creation.

Dr. Michael Flannery
Senior Lecturer in Education (Visual Arts), Marino Institute of Education

Leonard, Parzival and Pushkin

As a singer and songwriter I thought I got involved with the Pushkin Trust to help encourage young people to be creative. However, my Pushkin moment doesn't concern anybody else's creativity but mine.

I was working at a Pushkin event with a team of talented people and a whole clatter of student teachers from all over Ireland. Lindsay Clarke's beautiful BBC Radio 2 programme of his modern version of the Holy Grail story was the centre of the experience. We all listened to the dramatization of the story and then went into small groups to explore what we had gained from the hero's story. I think it was on the third episode when I had an epiphany. A few weeks earlier I had started a song after hearing a radio interview with Leonard Cohen. The interviewer asked Leonard what he thought of Elvis Costello saying;

> *There are about five things to write songs about:*
> *I'm leaving you. You're leaving me. I want you. You don't want me.*
> *I believe in something. Five subjects and twelve notes.*

Leonard replied,

> *Well maybe there's more, maybe there's less, but I think it's all gain and loss, victory and surrender.*

So I had the start of a song …

> *Leonard Cohen said it's all gain and loss*
> *Victory and Surrender*
> *I surrender*
> *Some times you win some times you lose*
> *Always a loser and a winner*
> *Saint and sinner …*

So I had the bones of the song but couldn't come up with a chorus that would make sense until I heard on Lindsay's programme that the times when Parzival found the Grail Castle was when he let the reins of his horse hang loose. Epiphany! That's it! I couldn't wait to get to the small group and get my guitar to get the thought in my head out into the world. I think the students thought I was a wee bit bonkers as I struggled to make the words and the music fit. Now it all made sense, the song's about giving up the notion that your ego is in charge of anything! And now the chorus goes ...

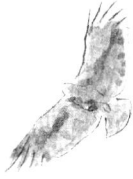

Let the reins hang loose cowboy.
Let the reins hang loose
Life will take you there if you let
Let the reins hang loose.

Don't fight the tide the moon always wins
Lose the war but win the battle
Another battle.

Don't try to make it rhyme just don't lose yourself
Hold on tight to things that matter
Love's all that matters.

If I lose you now it'll be a crying shame.
Who would I sing this song for
sing this song for?

Leonard Cohen said it's all gain and loss
Victory and Surrender
I surrender.

So let the reins hang loose, cowboy …

I was able to sing the song for the assembled company that evening and the students were heard singing it on the bus back to the B&B. My thanks to Leonard and Parzival and Pushkin.

Roy Arbuckle
Singer-songwriter

Inspiring Educators

To meet the needs of their pupils and to design, deliver and evaluate a challenging, motivating and exciting curriculum I believe that a teacher needs to be the most creative person in their classroom.

Yet when do teachers get the time to develop and enhance their own creativity? All too often any support and training which is provided only meets their professional needs and the personal development is forgotten.

Teachers need to be nurtured too. The Pushkin Inspiring Educators' Programme is designed to provide that personal development, that nurturing. It allows teachers to become in touch with the child within again, to refresh and replenish themselves, to go back to the well to draw upon the creative spirit within them.

In this programme teachers from Northern and Southern Ireland work together in creative partnerships and learning communities. Meeting at Baronscourt they participate in creative and environmental workshops designed to unlock, explore and enhance their personal creativity. By engaging in the programme they have the chance to share practice and ideas, through dialogue and collaboration.

Working with the Pushkin facilitators means that the teachers expand their repertoire of creative strategies allowing them to enhance the planning and delivery of learning and teaching in their classrooms.

In some schools the impact of the work they have undertaken with the Trust has really become embedded and is obviously central to the ethos of the whole school. We identify and celebrate these schools through the Inspiring Educators' Programme. These schools are being awarded the new mark – 'Rewarding Creativity' in recognition of their commitment to the promotion of the personal creativity of the staff as well as the children.

By investing in schools and teachers the Pushkin Trust hopes to give a voice to the creative spirit found in each person who encounters the programme.

Anne McErlane
Programme Manager, Inspiring Educators' Programme

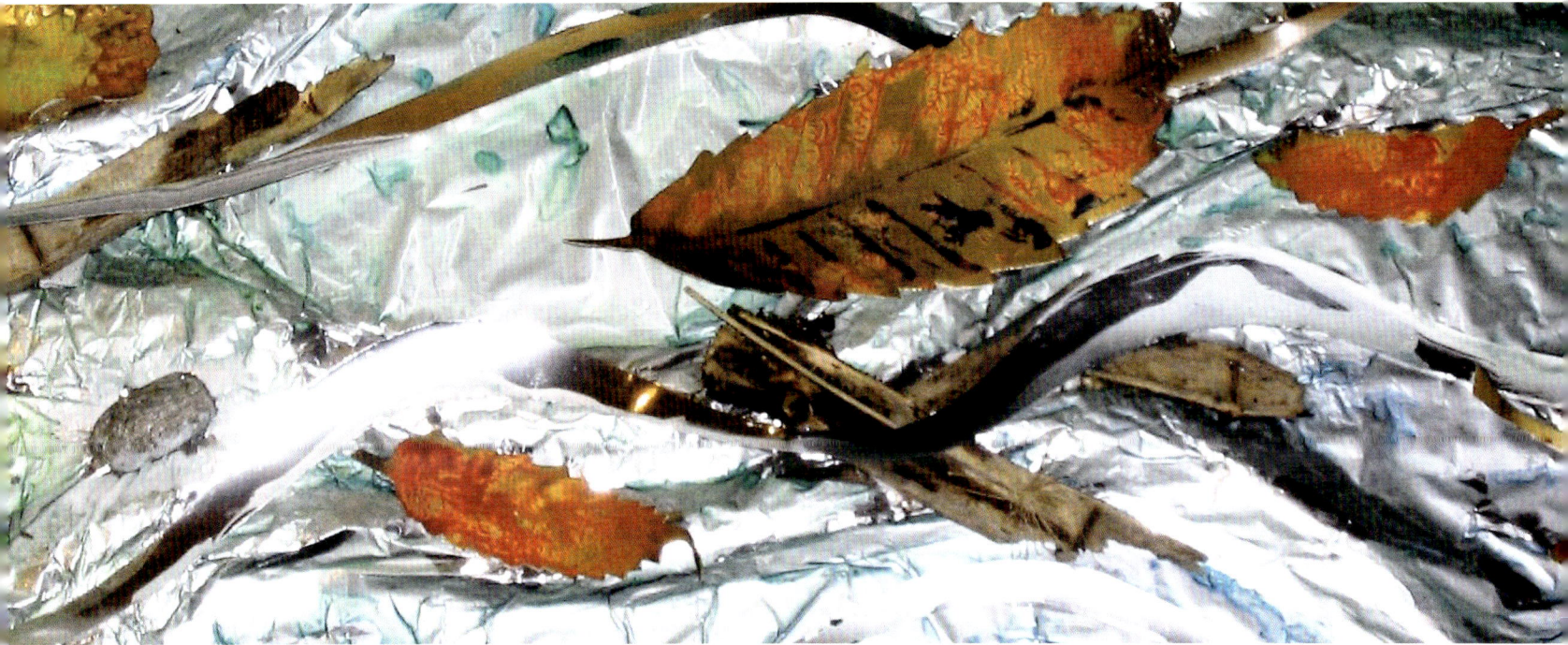

"At the Summer Camp of the Imagination, words float into music floats into dance floats into sculpture floats into the forest floats into us, making human beings of all of us."

New Roots

I write of love, death,
of life in the Big Apple.
I write of the pain of desperation,
of sorrow on leaving Ireland.
I write of walking along the sidewalks
mesmerised by twinkling lights.
I write of thunder, lightning, breaking dawn
when the Twin Towers broke with a yawn.
I want to write of innocent people,
hatred, strangers and Death Row.
I want to write of innocence,
of transforming experiences,
so you can hear of my new roots
sprouting in America.

Amanda Gallagher
Pupil

"...and
fingers
yearn for
pen..."

A New-Found Faith

You can't expect people to have faith in a religion unless they have an experience of it. Being the product of a third-level teacher education programme that valued the expression of learning as measurable, scientific and reason-based, it was refreshing to be rescued by an experience that characterised learning based on language, imagination and experience.

So as I presented for my first Pushkin workshop on writing poetry, our facilitator spoke about her life as a poet, the blocks she had to negotiate and the surge she felt when she got that image or word that had eluded her. She had a way; gentle, liberating and so naturally eloquent, an eloquence that was humble, inviting and accessible; powerful attributes to reassure the fledgling subjects who sat stiff around the navy-clad table. The blank page was confronted, the forgotten-self poured on to the Killyhevlin headed note paper and we passed through the Red Sea of our own fears and vulnerability, safe in the hands of our own Moses, Noelle Vial. The liberation was complete.

Paraig Cannon
Teacher

"Now strike your note..."

Let Some Sunlight In

The inky blackness blots out everything.
Gloomy monsters lurk in the crannies,
moaning and groaning,
stirring up vile potions
to blot out all light.
Open up the curtains!
Open up the curtains and let
the small golden fairies dance and flit!
Let their dainty golden wings
reflect rainbows on the ceiling,
squeeze curling wisps of lights
into every shadowy nook.
Let some sunlight in!

Molly Goyer Gorman
Pupil

"I found I had a talent for writing."

Symbol of Hope – A Visit to Russia

My perception of the Soviet Union had been coloured by images of grey buildings, grey, grim-faced men in fur hats and scenes of tanks, guns and hardware under grey October skies. I had thought of it as a sunless, cheerless, Godless place. We had prayed for its conversion in school and when I'd misbehaved as a small child my father had sometimes threatened to send me there. It was with mixed feelings, therefore, that I set off in June 1990 which was, for me, a journey into the unknown.

Russia is a country of contrasts. I will never forget the beauty and splendour of Moscow where every church and palace, throne, tower and tomb, whispers its testimony to glorious days and darkest nights. We wandered under the golden domes of the Cathedral of the Annunciation with its priceless icons where the Czars prayed, to the Cathedral of the Assumption where the Czars were crowned, to the Cathedral of St. Michael which contains tombs of Princes, Czars and other imperial dignitaries.

We visited a 'living church' when we were there – the Church of the Epiphany in outer Moscow. We lit candles and placed them at the priceless icons as priests and people prayed and chanted their way through a ceremony which seemed to be without end. The ladies all had their heads covered to contain the energy which is collected in church and wore black as an expression of obedience to God. It was a sunny Sunday morning and there we were – Protestants and Catholics from Northern and Southern Ireland brought together through Pushkin in a Russian Orthodox Church, united in Christianity.

The most memorable day of our trip for me was a visit to a little village, Zaharovo, about thirty kilometres from Moscow. We were greeted on our arrival at the village by a colourful throng of people – young men and women in local costume, chanting, singing, dancing, bringing ceremonial bread and salt for the Duchess and welcoming her as a Royal visitor, a link with the past, a reminder of something to which these country people held on tenaciously. We made our way to an old decaying church, where, in the graveyard, a group of priests had gathered (illegally) to hold a ceremony in memory of a dead ancestor of the Duchess. Again, the prayerfulness of the people, their deep faith and reverence was awe-inspiring.

In the school house we were served high tea from beautiful samovars, accompanied by all kinds of Russian sweetmeats, and the children of Ireland and the children of Russia exchanged gifts and communicated, despite the language barrier, as only children can.

This was a village of happy, smiling country people with a welcome for the stranger as warm and generous as one could ever experience. Here was a place that communism had not penetrated and where the simple joys of the common people of Pushkin's beloved Russia were indeed a 'Symbol of Hope.'

Shiela McCaul
Pushkin Trustee

82

АЛЕКСАНДРУ СЕРГѢЕВИЧУ

ПУШКИНУ.

Dear Denise,

The DVD arrived at mum and dad's so I will see it the next time I'm home. Thanks again for sending it. I promised to send you a paragraph about the importance of the Pushkin Prize for James.

There can't be many little boys from farms in Northern Ireland who travel to Russia, even today. But just at the end of the Cold War, in 1990, my little brother, James, aged 11, was exploring Red Square and buying Russian dolls in Leningrad, which was yet to be renamed St. Petersburg! He travelled with the Pushkin Trust, having won a prize for creative writing. There is poetry in the fact that the Trust works to give little kids in Northern Ireland an opportunity for self-expression, and they travelled to a place where self-expression had been long repressed. Over 1,500 miles from home in the heart of the Soviet Union, he wouldn't have understood the importance of 'glasnost' and 'perestroika', or how the world beneath his feet was shifting.

After he came home, James told how he had gotten lost in Moscow. "What did you do?" we asked him "I sat down and prayed," he said. "Then I found a policeman." So the policeman drove him around the neighbourhood and quickly located the rest of his group. This story would be recounted at his funeral just two years later. James died suddenly, aged thirteen, from an undetected cardiac condition. I will always be grateful to the Pushkin Trust for giving such a bright, energetic child the opportunity to shine, to explore and to grow.

I hope this is useful to you, Denise.

Best regards,
Alison

*"The Pushkin Trust makes all people kin.
It makes all our hearts keen."*

The Russian Dimension

I remember the day when my husband and I were looking for the small country, Ireland, in the Atlantic Ocean, on the map. It was July, 1993. Writing this article I am surrounded by a number of reminders which can tell many stories – stories which revive events connecting Russia and Ireland and my part in the Pushkin project. Here I see annual brochures of the Pushkin Trust's Schools' Programme, the book, *Eager we are to Live* – writings by children of Ireland and Russia for the Pushkin Prizes, *Snow in Summer* – writing by teachers for the Pushkin Trust, correspondences from Sacha, The Duchess of Abercorn herself, and *The First Great Book of the Pushkin Trust Russian Summer Camp of the Imagination, Roshchino 2005*. The Russian Summer Camp was a residential held in a forest outside St Petersburg and involved student teachers from St. Petersburg Pedagogical University working bilingually with a dramatist, a writer, a visual artist and a singer. This culminated in a public performance, and led to the pilot project, Pushkin Awards 2005 at the Derzhavin Museum, attended by the Duchess.

Many children from different schools in St. Petersburg were involved in the project. They developed and enriched their imagination, writing stories and poems during the school year and on a number of occasions the schools in Russia were visited by the Duchess and Irish teachers and writers. Some of the Russian children visited Ireland to attend the Summer Camp of the Imagination at Baronscourt, where they were able to converse and take part in creative writing in English – their second language. I think the link with the Russian Department of Queen's University, Belfast and Professor Marcus Wheeler was a very useful contact.

When I talk to the former students of the project they say that their participation was important for them in many ways. They had the chance to get acquainted with beautiful Ireland, its culture, very hospitable people, their customs and traditions. They learned to watch and better understand nature, and they became more creative. Now they are journalists, teachers, managers, doctors, scientists. It is interesting that all the experiences the children had with the Pushkin project were owing to the great Russian poet, Alexander Pushkin, and his direct descendant, Sacha Abercorn.

Now it is 2013. We have overcome the difficult '90s. We have become stronger, kinder and more patient. By taking part in the Pushkin project we have helped to keep the souls and hearts of our children open for the beauty of nature and regard for the planet.

I was very little. We visited an Art Studio and teacher asked us to draw a sun.
Every child made the sun orange yellow but my sun was black.
'Why? Why is it black? Sun must be yellow.'

Dasha Fomicherva

Memory is a bad servant.
Mind is unreliable.
But a heart is open for love
In spite of distance.

Composite poem, Roshchino 2005

Antonina Kosjakina
Teacher – Kolpino, St. Petersburg

The Tale of Pushkin House

It is, perhaps, apt that a building which was to be the architectural manifestation of the Pushkin Prizes, whose main thrust was to allow children, in the midst of sectarian repression and bigotry, to find their voices and unleash their imaginations, should begin with an idealistic dream. In 1998 the brief for the Pushkin House was ambitious. What was envisaged was a building containing a reception area, six workshop rooms, an IT Centre, a storytelling room, the Pushkin Library, a conference room, a dining room and offices. But more than these dry, spatial requirements, it would be warm, welcoming, spiritual, non-institutional and have something of the magic of Pushkin's stories, a stimulation to the imagination.

I took the brief at its face value. I enjoyed building the models of a couple of innovational, Pushkin-story-inspired schemes at that time. But then there was a three-year hiatus, a time of reflection for Sacha after which it was decided to move the site deeper into the Baronscourt coniferous forest, to reduce the scale of the building and to perhaps echo some reference to the dacha where Pushkin spent much of his childhood and where his beloved Babushka had filled his imagination with folk tales of Mother Russia. To acquaint me with and to remind Sacha of its specific vernacular architecture, there was a ten-day trip to Russia. It was nothing ordinary.

South of Novgorod is the outdoor Vitoslavlitsy Museum of Wooden Architecture, where buildings threatened in their original location are dismantled and brought in for protection. Here we found very relevant inspiration. The buildings were modest, simple and redolent of Pushkin's tales. There was a wooden church, St. Nicholas, I seem to remember, which had a lofty octagonal space over the iconostasis, with light piercing dustily from high windows. I remembered Sacha's description, three years before, of her desire to give children a sense of finding their centre, their voice and their spirituality. This space had that sort of focus. Somehow, our pilgrimage had found its landing place.

On the way back to St. Petersburg we stopped at a traditional wooden cottage where the old lady working in the garden, on hearing that Sacha was a descendant of Pushkin, picked all her gladioli and presented them to her, a huge armful.

Our inspiration from the loftiness of St. Nicholas Church bore fruit and I designed a new, smaller Pushkin House, the plan symmetrical on both axes with the central space rising to a square lantern. The floor level was raised above the ground about four feet, like we had seen at Vitoslavlitsy. I built a little balsa-wood model and Sacha was enchanted. She found a Shaman. He suspended his sensitive crystals over the site and they showed the exact spot where the crossing of my two axis lines would acquire most harmony.

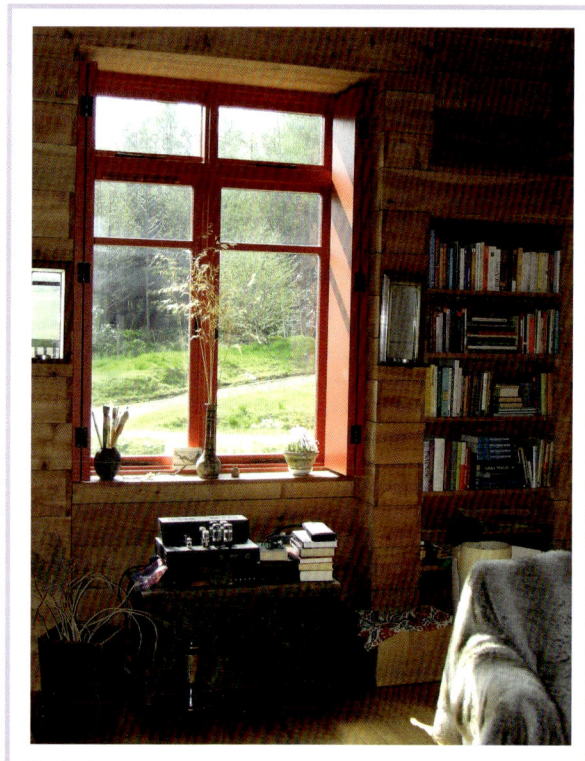

A local builder, Jack Lynch, who has been building for the Abercorns for decades was the man entrusted with the job of constructing Pushkin House. In this little corner of paradise the foundations were dug and dreams began to turn into reality. The first excitement was the sense of elevation and panorama from the raised floor level. The view out over the valley to the parkland beyond, punctuated by majestic old trees, is magical.

The house, as it has emerged, is clustered round the great central space. Everything is wood: the eight steps up to the entrance, the wide, welcoming door with its wrought iron plate behind the handle, copied from a church in Vitoslavlitsy, the warm, dark entrance hall which soars up to the underside of the steep roof, Sacha's sitting room, with its red shutters and bookshelves. In both this room and the central, gathering space are fireplaces based loosely on the plastered stoves we found in the Russian countryside. These are plainer. There's a little kitchen and shower-room. An open, roofed veranda wraps itself round the side to the view. Even the smell of the building is resinous. Sacha has covered her sitting room walls with small, Russian paintings, mostly landscapes. The comfortable chairs and sofa are covered with shawls, both patterned and fur. It really does look like a dacha!

In the central, focal room there are five large windows set in deep reveals with shutters and window seats. I hoped that the insides of the shutters might be painted by an artist, and suggested Noreen Rice. In discussions between Sacha and Noreen, it was agreed that the work should represent a threshold or bridge between two worlds, between the inner and outer landscapes. It could be like a door between the human and the divine; showing how creativity brings us from the dark into the light and also a reflection of the four elements with earth and fire and reflections of water and air flowing through.

For me having shared the happy tale of the Pushkin House with Sacha, Jack Lynch and Noreen Rice and all the other characters along the way has enriched my life and left its mark on the story of my own voice.

Richard Pierce
Architect of Pushkin House

Cúchulainn goes to Moscow and finds Kolobok

Thanks to a heady mix of serendipity and Anne McErlane's keen eye for forging creative partnerships, we were introduced almost three years ago to Alex Shcherbacheva from State Education Center 1329, in Moscow. Thus our Russian adventure began.

Initially we decided that we would research and share folks tales and legends from each other's countries. We submitted a number of legends including *The Children of Lir* and *The Salmon of Knowledge*. However when we introduced the Russian children to *Cúchulainn*, they were captivated. He became their hero. Their first response was to capture and retell our version of how he got his name as a series of images with bi-lingual subtitles in a PowerPoint presentation.

My class watched this in a glow of self-satisfied Celtic superiority, that is, until we came to the slide where Cúchulainn makes his first appearance. He had been interpreted as a leather-jacketed, comicbook, urban hero. Uproar and outrage ensued, calmed only by my observation that no disrespect was intended. Indeed the Russian children were only responding to the version of the story that they had been given by us.

Order was restored when our Russian friends asked us to script the story as a play for them to perform for their school. Using our own 'culturally correct' images, we created a movie, adding a sound podcast with assistance from the Nerve Centre. This was dispatched to complement the script we had prepared. We then had the entertainment of watching the performance from Moscow via the C2k videoconference platform, *Elluminate*.

Using movie-making techniques we had acquired from the Nerve Centre trainers we created movies to illustrate the Russian legends of *Father Frost* and *Kolobok*. Our Russian friends were enchanted by our interpretations. The story of *Kolobok* provided us with some entertainment. Originally, the story was sent to us in Russian and as the translation came to us by degrees, it provided a very interesting opportunity for prediction. One child was able to decipher the form of the story and declared correctly that the story of *Kolobok* was a version of our own tale of *The Gingerbread Man*; that naive and vulnerable sour dough creation who was at the mercy of more wily creatures.

Still smarting at the leather-jacketed insult to Cúchulainn, some of my boys scoured the Internet for a suitable revisionist image of Kolobok on which to base their movie. They were delighted to find a cigar-smoking, gun-toting and no-nonsense version that was anything but vulnerable.

On the whole, the exchange we enjoyed was challenging, innovative and hugely entertaining. The children used and developed a wide range of UICT and communication skills as they moved between media to craft an expression for their interpretations. New pathways were forged, new links with Russia and the children's creative output found expression in a variety of different media to draw ever closer to the home of his descendant the land of Pushkin.

Peter Heaney
Teacher

A View from Russia

I travelled from a Teacher Training University in Russia in March 2012 to come to a wonderful place in Ireland, my first time in this country. I'd never been to such a place and still think that everything that has happened to me is just a miracle, like a chapter from the fairytale. Anne and Alexandra were like kind fairies and we were the people for whom a little door to the magic world had been opened. I hope that for us this door will never be closed. After the words I've heard, the people I've met, the places and actions I've seen, I was shocked, I was amazed as I've never thought that people could be so, so really kind and sincere. I don't want to say that here in Russia we have a lack of all these qualities, but I would like to have more good qualities like you have in Ireland. After this trip some of my life views have changed for the better and I started to think that all over the world you can change people for the better like you did me. You are doing very worthy things and I hope that nothing will turn you from this path – this is the world path. If I were an artist I'd draw all the people I've met. If I were a writer, I'd write a novel. But I'm a beginning poet and singer and I have an idea inside me. Maybe someday I'll write a song about this magic week in green, green Northern Ireland and the world will listen to it, listen to my feelings and to my heart.

The Pushkin Trust makes all people kin. It makes all our hearts keen.

Anastasya Skoromnaya
Student Teacher

"I never realised I had so many dreams until I began to write them down."

A Memorable Visit to Pushkin's Petersburg

My years as a Trustee of the Pushkin Trust are full of the happiest memories. I felt part of a family of extraordinarily generous and dedicated people. That we had a sense of belonging to a family is not surprising since the Trust got its name from and was inspired by Alexander Pushkin, the ancestor of Sacha, Duchess of Abercorn, herself the inspirational founder of the Pushkin Trust. While being involved in the Pushkin schools programme, first as a judge and later as a Trustee, I met exceptional people who became and remain friends. Sadly some of our fellow Trustees have left us since and I think of them with affection, respect and a genuine sense of loss. They are still part of the Pushkin family however and their memory remains green – literally – as a tree has been planted in memory of each one beside the Pushkin House in Baronscourt.

At our quarterly meetings we Trustees dealt with serious educational and social matters in the most responsible ways but the tenor of those meetings was not gloomy or despairing. Though we met throughout the very worst of 'The Troubles' everyone remained positive, committed and hopeful. The other Trustees were busy people, many with high-ranking jobs that carried a considerable amount of responsibility, but their willingness to undertake extra work for the Trust was exemplary.

Over the years we had many happy times in Baronscourt but the outstanding memory of my time as Trustee was in 2003 when we went to St. Petersburg. It was the 300th anniversary of that beautiful city and it had been given a facelift so it was more beautiful than ever. As a direct descendant of the great writer, Sacha was looked on with awe by many of the people we met. This sense of a real connection with the writer enlivened the whole trip for me. It had the effect on *me* of making all the sites connected with Pushkin more real, less the stuff of literature only. That sense was most powerfully present on the occasion of our visit to the Lycée that Pushkin had attended in Tsarskoe Selo. On that day, at the annual commemoration of the founding of the Lycée, Sacha read poems from her collection of prose poems, *Feather from the Firebird*, proving herself a writer of real talent. She also laid flowers in honour of her legendary ancestor at the Pushkin memorial.

Of all the significant and memorable visits we made during our time there – a trip to see the Bronze Horseman, which inspired one of Pushkin's best known poems, the visit to the Pushkin Museum where we heard the young singers of the Mariinsky Theatre singing Pushkin songs – the event of the greatest relevance to us as Trustees was our visit to two schools in the city who were using the Pushkin blueprint in their curriculum. I felt that the Pushkin Trust had found the second home that the Duchess of Abercorn had envisaged from the start.

We were very impressed by the work being done in these schools while noting with interest the cultural differences between the Irish and the Russian methods.

As well as a total immersion in Pushkin's Petersburg we availed of the other cultural riches of this extraordinary city. We saw a performance of *Les Sylphides* in the Mariinsky Theatre and were taken back stage to see the vast area that housed stage-shifting equipment that belonged to another era but was still in use there. We visited the Hermitage Museum and I was astounded to find myself in a room full of Rembrandts. We attended a Russian Orthodox evening liturgy in St. Nicholas Cathedral and were overawed by the grandeur of the cathedral and the devoutness of the crowds of people who stood patiently throughout the long ceremony.

As well as visiting churches, palaces, museums and monuments we visited excellent restaurants and enjoyed wonderful meals together. The communal apartments we shared also encouraged camaraderie and a sense of youthful adventure. We were blessed too in our guide who was extremely efficient and a fund of knowledge. By the time we left St. Petersburg I felt as if I had made a genuine connection with the city and the great poet who gave his name to the Trust, to which I felt privileged to belong.

Marie Heaney
Pushkin Trustee, 1993-2007

My Pushkin Memory

It is really a challenge to put the Pushkin experience into words because for me it was something which has to be experienced. Being a guest in Baronscourt I felt at home, at ease, as if I were already part of the project which is reaching its twenty-fifth year. I believe that this place and project is not only for those who lack creative skills in their studies, job or life but also for those who want to experience new horizons, for people to learn something more than they already know about themselves. Personally, I have never seen such a devoted and inspired person as Sacha – that was how we were asked to address the Duchess – who let us into her own fascinating world full of inspiration, creativity, love for children, imagination and new incredible ideas amongst other things. She is the one to be thanked and appreciated for her work in inspiring others by opening up new ideas. I found myself in a magical world where the nature, the people, the atmosphere were so welcoming that leaving Baronscourt and those people, to whom we got deeply attached during such a short period of time, turned out to be a hard task. Now I feel like going back there to gain more experience and to contribute to that incredible project.

Oksana Pashyan
Student Teacher

"Pushkin was a friend to everybody who has done this work ...
Pushkin was a friend to me."

How Can I Keep from Singing?

I come from a family of talkers and storytellers. I think that is why I immediately connected with the work of the Pushkin Trust – an organisation which values the individual voice so much. Over the past twenty-five years Pushkin has been responsible for bringing thousands of people together in the name of 'finding a voice.' Through the experience of Pushkin, participants of all ages have been called forth into a new way of being, to a place of greater integration between the head and the heart and closer to a semblance of 'wholeness.' Participants' outward journeys to Pushkin workshops have mirrored inward journeys towards the depths of the soul.

Professor Ken Robinson, in his book *The Element – How Finding your Passion Changes Everything* speaks of how we are most ourselves, most inspired and achieve at our highest level when we find ourselves 'in our element.' That is an expression we use in my family. Another expression I use is 'on song.'

I have never been more 'on song' than when I have been engaged with the work of the Pushkin Trust. For me, it makes my whole life sing. So do I know 'A Song of Pushkin?' It is the melody and clear timbre of children's voices, singing from their souls, delight on their faces, their minds and hearts open to new possibilities. I have heard this melody.

Do I know 'A Song of Pushkin?' It is the way I have been transposed from one life to another by shifting provinces and perspectives, through journeying with others, alike and different, inspired and inspiring. It is the harmony found in meeting like-minded people and all the wonderful layers of garnished experience in creative spaces. I have hummed this melody.

Do I know 'A Song of Pushkin?' It is the cadences of poetic speech, being lost in the majesty of the written word amid the guiding voices for Pushkin – the writers and torch-bearers of the Pushkin flame – as I endeavoured to be the scribe for the Pushkin story.

In the words of the Enya song;

I hear its music ringing
It sounds an echo in my soul
How can I keep from singing?

Helen Slattery Cannon

Survival

A polar bear.
Prowling precariously,
Waiting for some food.
In the surge of the sea,
He sees a seal.
Without a doubt,
He jumps right in.
A baby seal is an easy target –
It can hardly swim.
The polar bear bites the seal –
His sharp jaws snap shut …
the seal is dead.
The bear can feast –
His tummy yearns no more.

Curtis Burgess
Pupil

The Mild Winter

All mixed up!
Not quite sure
If they should hunt or hibernate,
The little hedgehogs can't decide
If they should sleep or stay awake.

He starts. He stops,
He starts again, building his nest.
The silly old crow,
He doesn't know
What time of year it is.

The little shoots of daffodils are up too soon,
The buds on trees appear,
The cows and sheep are mixed up too,
What is this time of year?

Cathy Gormley
Pupil

The Simple Truth

Educators from all over Ireland have paid tribute to the ability of Pushkin to inspire. Teachers and pupils have described how their contact with this movement helped to unlock in them a creative potential which they never knew existed. Such hidden treasure inside themselves might always have lain dormant in their normal school lives but was triggered into life and has never left them since. They attribute this life-changing experience to a specific occasion when the magic of Pushkin worked in them. Obviously, such talk of 'magic' is dangerous. So much has to happen before and after any such educational success story can happen. But it is experienced by those to whom it happens as an instantaneous occurrence. It takes longer to ensure that the initial experience is cultivated and that it endures. But the process may begin over a few days. For maximum impact and long-term effect it takes time to develop. There has to be the possibility to tap back into the source of inspiration again and again. When we talk of 'magic' in terms of the Pushkin process or any other pedagogical method we have to be careful. It seems to describe some quick-fix programme which provides a child with powers that are otherwise unavailable. The truth is more simple. Every child has a wealth of imagination which comes naturally and is often expressed in games and behaviour patterns usually ignored by the adult world. The systems of education which we have inherited, and to which most of our children are exposed systematically, stifle all such playful virtuosity. The answer to the question how we promote imagination in our children is so simple that it can be overlooked. We don't have to do anything, it is already there, it only has to flourish. We don't have to promote it, we only have to remove the obstacles we have put in its way and allow it time and the ambiance conducive to its display of itself.

Providing the atmosphere and the channel for the imagination is the magic of Pushkin. And this 'magic' has now been practiced so often and has achieved such startling success, especially with students who were regarded as underachievers in their own school environment that the organizers have been able to analyse the process and describe in slow-motion how it happens. Its effect is palpable after the experience, not just with children but more importantly with teachers and parents who sometimes accompanied their children and were reluctantly dragged into the magic circle even though they had intended to remain outside observers. Essential to the Pushkin experience is the joy of discovering the unique imprint which we can all make, that no one else can make no matter how faltering or inadequate that contribution may prove to be objectively. It is the taking of these initial steps, however fumbling or ungainly, which open the sluice gates to further imaginative endeavour. These tentative steps and the ensuing confidence which they bring are the essential permission we need to further explore our imaginative capacities. And this confidence spills over into all aspects of our lives and our work.

Mark Patrick Hederman
Author and Abbot of Glenstal Abbey

The Classroom Visit

An oppressive blanket covers and smothers us as we anticipate the arrival. The boisterous but inoffensive banter, ear cuffing, teasing, slapping and flirtatious whistling that usually trumpet the entrance of 10A1 are absent. Josh, eyes scanning the arena, was even more uncommunicative than usual.

The Magi enter. Chilli peppers sizzle on tongues, fingers and nostrils. Father Sun and the element of fire are real and vibrant. Sloppy copies feel the weight and speed of ideas, memories and stories. Their voices warm and swell, feeding and pushing the flame from head to hand. Desperate for attention and an audience, they share, warmed by the heat of their ideas and each other's. To the outsider it is a dank, dragging, achingly-boring school day but the opening rays of Father Sun toss our blanket aside as upturned faces accept the spiking heat of inspiration.

Josh has words on a page. Instinctively Her Grace's antennae detect his reluctance but she invites him to read: "Josh … what economy of language. Beautiful."

His face cracks open. I swear I can hear a purr emanating from the base of his throat. His voice flies unfettered.

Josh went on to become Head Boy three years later.

Pearl Stewart
Programme Manager, Pushkin Pathway Project

"We passed through the Red Sea
of our own fears and vulnerability …"

'Where I come from'

I come from Gortnatraw
where I belong.

I come from a family of five,
where I am loved and cared for.

I come from a fairy tale,
that's never been told.

I come from a game of chance
that goes on forever.

I come from a song,
where the words have no end.

I come from a secret
of friendship.

I come from a deadly game
and I am the girl who was on fire.

I come from a box,
filled with sparkles and diamonds.

I come from a world
of colour and magic.

I come from a poem,
which gives me a passion to write.

I come from the alphabet,
so I can spell I.

I come from numbers,
and I am the number one.

I come from the light in the sky,
the heavens smiling at me.

I come from a cupboard of sweets,
marshmallows, crisps and chocolate.

I come from bubble gum,
strawberry, apple and mint.
That is where I come from.

Duyen Jones
Pupil

*"I never knew so much creative
writing could be so much fun."*

At Annaghmakerrig's Door

It was a sunny Sunday afternoon in July. I was driving down the tree-lined lane to Annaghmakerrig, wondering what lay in store, for I had booked in for a week-long course in creative writing. A smiling Helen Slattery welcomed me and showed me to 'Miss Warby's' room. Wow – this was different – like going back to my Granny's parlour. The view of the lake from the window looked inviting. Downstairs two other would-be writers had arrived. Frances from Dundalk and Alan from Belfast and both thought it would be nice to go for a walk by the lake. And so we did, exchanging introductory thoughts about why we had come.

Well what a transforming influence that experience was to be! By the end of the week we were firm friends and I was totally hooked on the Pushkin dream thanks to the poetic rhyming of Sandy Brownjohn, the creative sensitivity of writer Siobhán Parkinson and the often hilarious drama classes with John McArdle. And in between the writing there were the unforgettable meals around the big table, delightful conversation, friendly banter and food fit for a king. At night, after dinner, sitting around the fire there were sing-songs, party pieces and rib-tickling entertainment for as long as you could stay awake!

The week ended with the traditional reading of our creative pieces. I surprised myself because I had written a story. I drove out the tree-lined lane on Friday evening eager to share the Pushkin possibilities with my class and my colleagues. The door was more than open now.

Kitty Hughes
Pushkin Regional Leader

"The Pushkin project let me feel free."

"I learned I could write things about myself instead of keeping them locked up inside."

The Redwood Tree

"So, who wants to hit the tree?" I asked.

Before me were ten bemused children and their teacher, unsure whether they had understood the question, or the accent of the environmentalist. One boy was not even entirely convinced it was even a real tree but instead a Hollywood plastic stand-in from a movie set.

The ancient redwood towered above us. Green frond-like branches draped down towards us and the mottled spongy bark glistened red ochre in the crisp, spring morning.

"Is anyone learning to play the drums?" I asked.

A scattering of hands went up and this time the 'tree sceptic' boy stepped forward towards the tree with a little apprehension. Before him the tree soared to over sixty metres and if the whole group had held hands we could barely have made a circle around it.

"Hit the tree with the palm of your hand," I said "… and don't worry it won't hurt!"

The boy reached up and stuck the tree with his hand. A melodic boom reverberated around the group. There was a brief pause as the astonishment of the situation sank in. He quickly beat the tree again and again, as though the tree was now a large African drum and he had been transformed into a musical maestro. There was a large smile on his face, his eyes shone with wonderment and he muttered the universal Tyrone word children used when impressed; "Class!"

"Can I have a go?" echoed a chorus of eager children and before long Baronscourt was alive with the music of children and nature, interconnected and intertwined together by the creative arts. The redwood tree was now part of our group and everyone wanted to find out more about this majestic tree. A vital connection had been made that day with nature and it is one that will stay with these children and their teacher for a lifetime. The unique pairing of the environment and the creative arts is only delivered by the Pushkin Trust in Northern Ireland. The Pushkin Trust acts like a crucible, blending these usually widely divergent elements together, sprinkling its magic and producing nuggets of pure gold in *all* those who participate in it.

Lynn Greer
Environmentalist

The Fire Within

One of my most remarkable memories as Principal of Edenbrooke P.S. was the school's involvement in *The Fire Within* concert which was staged in the Waterfront Hall in May 2007. In that year *The Fire Within* was the inspiring theme of the Pushkin Trust's schools' programme and twelve primary schools in the greater Shankill area decided to collaborate and produce creative pieces befitting the Waterfront stage. The vision behind the concert was to showcase the talents of the children and by involving past pupils, who were positive role models, the whole Shankill area was sending out a clear message; that children from that area could achieve great things.

The theme engaged teachers but more importantly the pupils too. Pushkin facilitators worked in schools. The environmentalists took children to the local parks and places of interest. Artistic facilitators worked with pupils in dance, music, poetry, art and story writing. The University of Ulster joined the project and their art students worked with pupils to produce amazing backdrops for the Waterfront stage. The Belfast School of Music played a major role in assisting with the musical items. Arthur Webb, a Belfast Education and Library Board Advisor, coordinated the whole event. He worked tirelessly to ensure that the work produced was of the highest quality. He visited all the schools and the many challenges that had to be overcome were all surmounted through his careful direction and the cooperation of the staff from each school. There was widespread support from the community as everyone wanted their child to be on the 'big stage.' Messages of support came from President McAleese, Mrs Cherie Blair Q.C., Rt. Hon. Peter Hain, M.P., Gordon Brown and Baroness Blood.

So embracing the Pushkin theme that year found the whole Shankill community reaching out to the wider Belfast community. Children were enthused and that enthusiasm carried into their academic work too. Their parents became more involved in their children's school lives. They participated in poetry classes with renowned poet Adrian Rice and wrote some memorable poems. The whole of the Shankill celebrated the fact that there was a good news story coming from the area and not the usual negative comments. The biggest benefit was that the pupils and teachers involved were able to work together in harmony. Everyone involved became one large school community, one family, working for the greater good.

Pushkin has the power to transform lives, to engage pupils, parents and teachers in the creative process and thus make a difference.

Betty Orr
Pushkin Trustee, 2002-2012

Silence

The coils of the rope are hanging against the harbour wall. The lobster pots are stacked one by one. The trawlers' engines have stopped working. Shrill shrieking seagulls fly in circles above the harbour, waiting for the engines to start up and the fog of smoke to appear over the sky like a surrounding blanket, but the engines remain silent. The fish merchants are turned back and workers in the fish factory arc not at work today. They are paying their respects to Patrick Murphy who died last night trying to earn a living at sea.

Alan Laird
Pupil

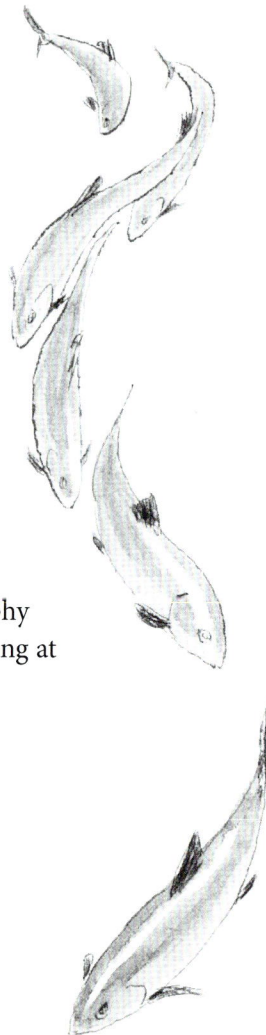

"We are made of seawater and stardust."

The Symbol of Hope

She has survived the mastectomy;
The draining, the depression, the nausea,
The trap of chemotherapy
When the drip haunted her,
Trailed her footsteps everywhere,
Followed her to the lavatory,
Listened to her talking,
Filled her plans,
Charted her future with shadows of uncertainty –
Shadows which would become the certainty of
two children.

Sixteen summers later
Still she fills people
With the light of hope,
Dispels the mystery of the crab
That crawls unseen,
Sometimes to flower,
Sometimes to die.

Ann Buckley
Teacher

"I am still writing stories in my spare time."

Sycamore Seeds

Sycamore seeds fall –
Helicopters twirling on
Their maiden voyage.

Gráinne Toomey
Pupil

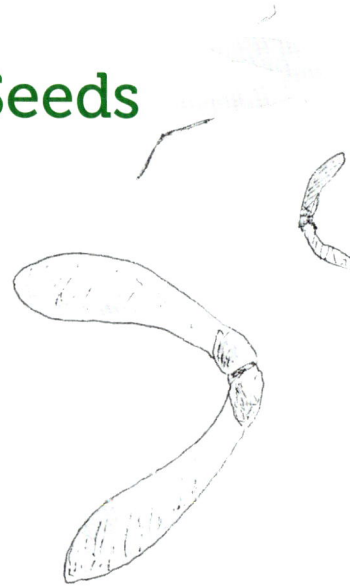

"The feeling of drowning in my imagination."

A Path to Sound

Tuning in our awareness to the natural world is a first step in attuning to a deeper sensitivity. Music, is an abstract artform. It cannot express semantically, but rather connects to deep-seeded colossi within ourselves: emotion, feeling, energy, colour, pace. Placing the natural world at the core of the Pushkin experience starts to align us with our own creativity. This is the first gift of the Pushkin programme.

The Pushkin walks allow for moments of stillness, letting the pace and feel of the environment impact on us, if we choose, rather than us simply impacting on it. Being silent in a forest, being sensitive and receptive to the natural world's sound and silence around us is an incredibly instructive and expansive gateway into exploration of the sonic.

I recently listened to the phenomenally gifted pianist Lang Lang advise: "You have to bring the whole planet into your interpretation …" My thoughts turned to Pushkin.

Pushkin offers to place *creation from nothing* at the heart of its artistic activity. Something that does not yet exist will form the response to immersion in the natural world. For most, not least children, celebration of music will almost exclusively be of learning pre-made songs, pre-made pieces, pre-made musicals. Everything arrives as a finished, pre-completed product, to be learned and rendered in performance. Nothing is being made from scratch. Nothing is being challenged. It all pre-exists. It's safe. The act of creating, as opposed to rendering performance of something already pre-existing, is a very different engagement. It fills the cracks you don't even realise are there. It opens to a perspective not found by any other means. It's like an explorer tackling the vast outback without a map.

Developing creativity runs concurrent with nurturing an openness, a receptiveness, dissolving preconceptions, drawing on intuition you might not yet even know you have. So much of what is most crucial to the Pushkin process develops beyond the immediacy of the piece or workshop at hand. The process is beautiful, it is subtle. In the longterm, I believe its enduring value is in carving new *songlines* of perception, which resonate long after any individual workshop or creation has come to a close.

Deirdre McKay
Composer

"Whatever happens, happens!"

So Many Memories

Some moments in time define the rest of our lives. Pushkin has defined both my personal and professional life since I first became involved in November 1997. My first weekend in Donegal town, meeting like-minded teachers and writers, began the sea-change in my life and started a timeline that has been populated with creativity, friendship and fun. The chance to work as a professional with the greatest artists and teachers and to be treated as an equal has changed my attitude to professional development. Involvement in all aspects of the Pushkin Prizes and later helping to shape and create the Pushkin Awards has left me with a bank of memories and a network of friends. Taking part in the Summer Camp of the Imagination, the Summer School for Teachers, having a piece of my writing published in an anthology, working as a Pushkin Regional Leader – all of these are such a huge part of my life.

When I reflect on my time in Pushkin, my mind floods with so many memories. I recall writing in the Log Cabin, the smell of the log fire and the sputtering sound of dozens of candles as I was transported back to my childhood; reliving memories that had been buried in my subconscious for years.

I hear myself composing music with Elaine Agnew and almost a hundred children, when we created the sound-scape of a rainstorm by simply using our fingers to drum on the floor in the stable yard – eerie, realistic and sensational. I remember the amazement of my colleagues when I was able to jump-start writer Charlotte Corey's car when she had run down her battery! I am returned to the evening when I sat beside the erudite Michael Longley, in a hushed and silent room, as he read and discussed his work.

However, one moment that stands out in all of my Pushkin memories happened in Annaghmakerrig at the Summer School for Teachers. We shared dinner each evening at the long, scrubbed, pine table, full of laughter, singing and stories. We worked hard day after day, giving our very souls in creative writing workshops. We had all strived to perfect our writing, drafting and re-drafting, agonising to find the best word, the perfect metaphor, but we turned into immature children when an inspector arrived! We could write and perform our work for others yet when an inspector was in our midst, all our confidence deserted us. As French novelist Honore de Balzac said "Sometimes at the best moments a single word or look is enough." We all looked at each other and we knew!

Mary O'Kane
Teacher and Pushkin Regional Leader, 2000–2007

"I had to dig down into my heart ... when I finally came up with something it was a sensational feeling."

The Fish

Splish, Splash, Oh! what a crash,
One wave after another.
The little fish went up and down
Along came his brother.

They heard a noise- there was a boat,
Fishing nets are near!
Danger, danger, swim, swim, quick!
Let's get out of here.

If we get caught, we're on a plate
battered and or fried.
No time to turn or we'll be gone
Split along the side.

Are we going to hide or not?
Can we get away?
Let's hide down under the rocks
Then head for the bay.

Ah! Peace at last to swim around
The water is so calm
Let's stay down very near the sand,
Where there will be no harm.

A shock to come- fishing rods about!
Too late now to flee.
A hook has caught my brother dear,
Oh! What's in store for me?

The fisherman throws his rod again,
I am so very near.
Unless I try to get away,
I'm caught- I fear.

Dianne Smyth
Pupil

"I could let my imagination run free."

"When you write stories and poems nothing is wrong.
I wrote some good pieces and I was well pleased with myself."

My Wish for Pushkin

The most wonderful thing about Pushkin is that it encourages and enables teachers to find time for themselves. In that space, I rediscovered the creative part of me that was essential to both my personal and professional life and which ultimately benefited my students in so many different ways.

Perhaps this is the elusive essence of Pushkin that we find hard to define. Pushkin recognises that good teachers are givers and that in giving to these teachers, they will become re-energised and will 'pay forward' all they have gained to the children in their care. Teachers tend to work in a vacuum. Once the classroom door is closed there is no real opportunity of communicating with another adult, never mind a writer. It's amazing how many teachers have never met any of the writers whose work they teach. That is why Annaghmakerrig and the November Conference were the most valuable experiences for teachers and the time spent meeting like-minded people and learning from them and from the talented facilitators was much appreciated by all who attended. The opportunity to meet and work with writers was very special. I'll never forget how the faces of the teachers and children lit up when Marita Conlon-McKenna walked into the room at a celebration in May 2009.

The creative writing exercises taught me much more than the obvious. In having to read my 'scribblings' to others I recalled what it is like to be a pupil in a classroom: shy, perhaps a little frightened of the reaction from the peer group and the teacher. In the past I never asked children to read their work aloud to avoid causing them embarrassment but thanks to the excellent Pushkin facilitators I learned how to handle these situations and now my students love reading their work and getting praise and even advice, from their peers. Creative writing soon became a favourite classroom activity. And, of course, another benefit comes in June when rather than fearing the dreaded Leaving Cert exam essay, the students actually look forward to it. Many of my students have achieved so much as a direct result of the Pushkin method both in exams and in the number of awards they have received. Several former students are now published authors.

I can never thank Sacha Abercorn enough for her great vision and for making it all a reality. Pushkin is truly a wonderful gift to the children and teachers of Ireland, North and South and it should be a role model for all education systems. My hope is that one day the Pushkin method will be firmly established in the hearts and imaginations of students and teachers around the world.

Hilda Quin
Teacher and Pushkin Regional Leader, 2000–2007

"... what an experience in life, literature and ourselves ..."

A 'Coming of Age' Celebration – The Waterfront Hall – 7th June 2005

In 2005, the Pushkin Trust hosted its 'Coming of Age' celebration and I was delighted to be there to be part of the event. Children and teachers from primary, secondary, special needs and Irish-medium schools from all over Ireland were involved. They were joined by a group of ten children and their teachers from St. Petersburg, who came specially to make their own contributions to the festivities. Seamus Heaney and Michael Longley were the guests of honour and the event was attended by many other friends from the literary and arts worlds.

I had personally been involved with the Pushkin Trust for many years, as one of a number of facilitators of creative workshops for diverse groups of people connected with Pushkin, including teachers and trainee teachers. I remember looking forward to seeing how this workshop work might have gone on to manifest itself through the children's creative work.

The results were beyond my wildest dreams and remain vividly in my mind. I will never forget the incredible exuberance and excitement of the children themselves and the wonderful vibrant aliveness and direct heartfelt creativity of the exhibition based on the theme of *Threads* which represented the voices of the children of Ireland, both Catholic and Protestant, north and south of the border. I felt it was very important that the work of the Pushkin Trust was made visible in this way, for the whole world to see and everyone to share. I also clearly remember the beautiful song and dance piece by the children from St. Petersburg.

During the years that I had been connected with the Pushkin Trust, I had also been doing research that was about exploring the voice of the feminine principle in the visual arts. The afternoon at the Waterfront made an important contribution to my research. It confirmed for me, the healing nature of creativity. It re-affirmed my belief in the need to connect or re-connect with our own inner child, our inner image-maker, and the ability to be able to allow that inner child to express itself in an authentic and spontaneous way.

In 2005, the Pushkin schools' programme, which had been established and developed over eighteen years, was scaled back to allow for new developments in the world of business and the wider community. Since then, the Pushkin Trust has continued to evolve and grow. The work of the Trust is visionary and hugely important in the way in which it encourages children to explore and express all aspects of themselves, to see from a distance, feel connectedness and find their authentic voices. In doing so, it is helping to create a new sort of human being that can start to heal some of the splits in our consciousness that have created such enormous problems for humanity.

Sue Michaelson
Artist, Writer and Workshop Leader

The Roots of Spring

Spring is here, finally some sun,
Buds pop up and hedgehogs come
out of the hiding place they've been,
and dance to the new season theme.
Flowers appear like out of nowhere,
And some people try their just-bought spring-wear.
It all comes from the January sales,
And farmers collect up all the bales.
Spring's like a blank canvas just filled with paint,
People hope the bad weather doesn't come late.
The children go outside again
and smell the flowers filled with scent.

Orla Duignan, Cara Gilliland, Jack Kelly
Pupils

"I might even be a poet when I grow up."

Journeying from Connectivity to Creativity through Pushkin

In my youth I asked a wise man: "How do I know when I'm in love?" He replied: "When you feel very comfortable in the loved one's presence." It was good advice! Being comfortable in the company of someone can lead to the growth of love.

Nowadays I ask, "Are children comfortable with the world around them?" I believe not. Many are disconnected from their surroundings because their lives are immersed in gadgetry which promotes inward perspectives and inhibits outer ones. Disconnectedness and apathy go hand in hand.

Recently I tested around a hundred bright young people on the names of ten common trees. The best I could get from them was two out of ten! This is only one example of many instances where I find that the knowledge and consequent appreciation of nature is non-existent or lacking amongst many young people. Surprisingly, they often know plenty about the duck-billed platypus or other non-native species. It's what's outside their own back-door that they find uninteresting and unappealing.

Knowledge of one's world is living in a full circle. Living in this circle leads to feeling comfortable with one's surroundings and eventually the love of all plants and 'all creatures great and small.' Pushkin has long promoted engagement with the environment as a springboard for healthy living and creative stimulus. Many children's and adults' lives have formed full circles as a result.

I have been privileged to witness the transformation myself many times. I saw children connecting with nature and sparking with creativity in tranquil places like Kilruddery House, Pakenham Hall and Marley Park. I also witnessed teachers and student-teachers becoming fully alive in such beautiful places as the Burren, Lough Eske, Glenstal Abbey, Baronscourt and St. Enda's Park.

Connectivity with nature leads to knowledge; knowledge leads to life-long alertness and creativity. All enhance mental health. Today's educators can learn a lot from the Pushkin approach.

Paddy Madden
Environmentalist, Historian and Lecturer, Coláiste Mhuire, Marino

"When I take the children out of the classroom
and into their local environment they enter a realm
where all kinds of things are possible ..."

The Right Word

for Larry Monteith

Put your ears to the trees … what can you hear?
Children and teachers move in to listen,
Touching each trunk like there's something to fear,
Their faces full of anticipation.
Then the shock as everyone fathoms
The hidden melody of living trees,
That sounds like they hold tremendous gallons
Thundering into invisible seas.
Both teachers and children gather themselves
To pen a few words to frame for the shelves
And walls of their classrooms and families.
One tough guy checks it was water he heard –
Same water that rolls through you and through me –
Then moves on, chuffed that he knew the right word.

Adrian Rice
Poet

*"The joy of discovering the unique imprint
which we can all make."*

My Place

I see the reflective sea
clear as a crystal ball,
Children splashing and frolicking,
The crashing water awaking you
from your sunbathing
like an alarm clock.

I see fields,
Fields of home,
Fields of length,
Fields of solitude
Making me ablaze
deep inside my heart.

I wish for the best.
I love my family and my friends.
And I remember Granny and Grandad.
Their warmth, cuddles and chat.

I see beauty and friendship.
I think of family and friends
worldwide.
I hope someday to see
Love and peace
throughout our Galaxy.

James McCollum
Pupil

"... whether we live north or south of the border we are all equals. The Pushkin Prize encourages this equality."

Enchantment Reigned

In my view enchantment is a much overused word. Its lustre is dulled by frequent use in less than enchanting circumstances. We all know what it means however, and each of us can recall a special experience that can be expressed in no other way.

A Pushkin event provided me with one such unforgettable occasion. Though the setting for the Silver Jubilee, in Belfast's delightful Opera House, is of itself conducive to wonderment, the event was more to do with people than place. As one of hundreds of Pushkin devotees, I was enjoying the enactment through conversation, storytelling, poetry, and drama of the stage show. The participation of school children alongside actors made for an interesting mix. Aware of the approaching interval I assumed that the show would be in two discrete halves; that the format presented would bring the first half to its conclusion.

Suddenly the stage filled with a tide of children – running, spinning, rolling, linking hands, intermingling, separating, sweeping this way and that, to a seamlessly choreographed routine. Dramatic intermittent lighting on simple black costumes added marvellously to the effect. It was, however, Katie Melua's hauntingly beautiful voice that transformed the spectacle: enchantment reigned. The song *When You Taught Me How to Dance* seemed to carry the performance to an ethereal level.

So powerful was it that I actually found the experience uncomfortably emotional. As is often the case with disarming experiences, I had no idea where the intensity lay. I put it down to the magic of perfect art but felt that some other indefinable element was also subliminally at play. Analysis was for later, however, or not at all. For now I did not want the perfection to end.

The subsequent enthusiasm of the applause showed that I was not alone. I looked around at people rising to their feet clapping vigorously. To my right the Duke of Abercorn's warm facial expression revealed that he too had been enchanted.

Gordon D'Arcy
Pushkin Trustee, 2007–2012

"passionate fire, uncontainable..."

Drúcht an tSaoil

Drúcht na maidine
Drúcht na hoíche
Drúcht ar mo shúile
I mo bheola
I mo chroíse.

Máire Andrews
Teacher

*"Writing is no longer a chore but a chance
to explore inner and outer landscapes."*

Mum

My mum is:
A sick-bed soother
Likes to hoover
Neat and tidy
My mum is very bright.
I don't need to turn on the light
She likes to sleep (all the time)
So very, very deep,
She counts about twenty sheep
And she doesn't even make a peep.

She's a first-class shopper
Very sweet,
Gives out love
Just like a treat.
She really likes to hug a lot
But it's really, really tight.

She likes pups, kittens, and bunnies too
And after a bad performance she doesn't boo.
She hates noise,
And buys lots of toys,
She helps me with a really hard sum.

I just have to say, I love you mum.

Harry Grace
Pupil

The All-Embracing Spirit of Pushkin

I have a friend, Maurice Meehan, who is working with the Departments of Health and Education, to establish a project whereby young children are taught empathy. It seems to me that since 1987, when Sacha, Duchess of Abercorn, founded it, the Pushkin Trust has been doing just that.

So that at the first Summer Camp of the Imagination, Anna McCarthy, P6, could sit on a branch of the cedar of Lebanon and write in the cedar's voice:

> *I will bargain my shelter for your company.*

And Conor Parke, P5, when we had blindfolded ourselves to experience what it would be like to lack sight:

> *Your ears are your other eyes.*

Creative writing, wherever it is done, has to be fun. It has to be meaningful. It has to be devoid of cruelty. We all have to take risks – with language, and with what we reveal about ourselves, without what Beckett called "fraudulent manoeuvres" and without cliché. We have to sublimate the ordinary. We all have to know that we can use words to say whatever we need to.

> *So many words being made up each day I can't keep track of them.*
> *Little bullets of information shooting at each other.*
> *It's hard to find something that does not have a word.*
>
> Liam Morrow (5th class)

The Baronscourt Days and the Summer Camps have an extra dimension – the estate, with its forests and lakes, the Log Cabin with its open fire and candles (*There's a whole heap of darkness down here.* Michael, P6), and the truly, all-embracing spirit of the place.

A child from a school in North Belfast wrote: *My best day is being here with yous ones.* And it was salutary and moving to see each of them carefully tap their log on the floor before placing it on the fire, so that the woodlice would have a chance to escape. And in a world which places less and less value on the living, to see city children who might have been squeamish, reach forward with bare hands to place every last tadpole back in the water in case they dehydrated and died. I remember one boy who didn't want the day to end, who wanted to take it with him, and keep it with him (*Black smells like an old disused fireplace … Bats dream an upside-down universe*). His arms were full and his fists clenched on his gathered things. So that when night fell back in Belfast –

> *Night is like anything.*
> *Your imagination is in darkness.*
> *You see what you imagine.*
> *Even with your eyes open you can almost get*
> *lost in yourself …*

he would have with him a stick, a stone, a dead magnolia head, some leaves, and, I feared, a tadpole – and, I hoped, the words, and a knowledge that they were his to use. Because if you know your worth when you are nine, no one will ever be able to tell you otherwise.

Kate Newmann
Poet

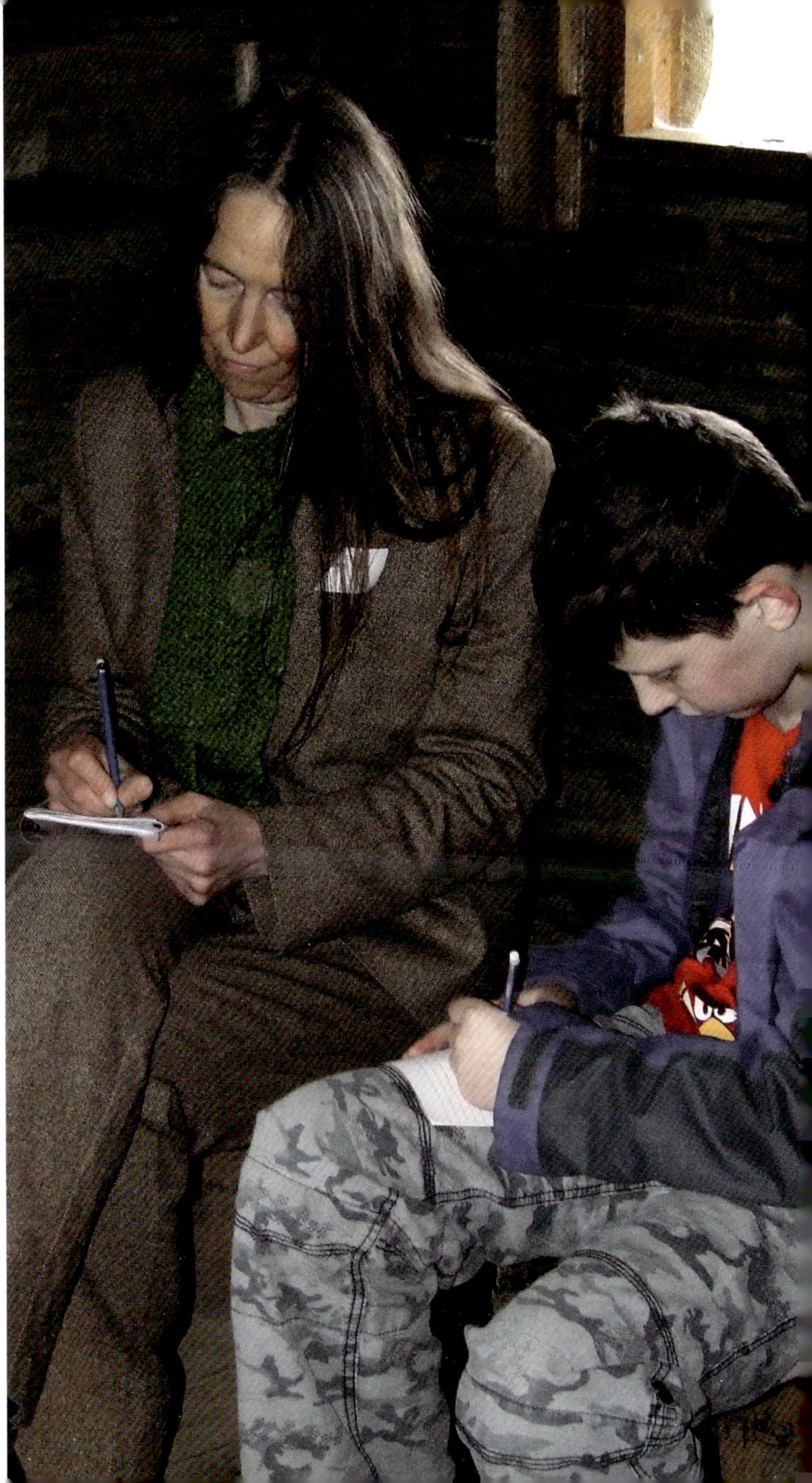

Reflections

Fifteen years before the Duchess of Abercorn established the Pushkin Trust in memory of her illustrious ancestor our third child died five hours after being born. This happened in a day when scant thought was given to the trauma young couples like us were going through without an emotional compass. We never saw or were offered the opportunity to hold 'Richard' and they even offered to "look after things" for us to avoid a funeral.

Some time later our thoughts turned towards adoption and it was natural to discuss the matter with friends who had been through the process twice. I will never forget what Gerry said to me as we neared the end of our exploratory chat, "… I hope you people have no vaulted ideas of what you might do for this prospective adoptee. It's not what you do for the child. It's what the child does for you."

I have spent many happy, thought-provoking and creatively-enriching years as a member of the Pushkin family. Those 'in charge' inspired us with a professionalism that was staggering. They were enthused, we teachers were enthused, so was it any wonder that the children we were privileged to teach were also inspired to reach heights neither they nor us could have imagined? 'There are some things that money can't buy' goes the TV advertisement, and this can be applied to Pushkin. But to re-echo and slightly re-arrange what Gerry said to me all those years ago;

"It's not anything that we have done for Pushkin, but what Pushkin, has done for us." The Pushkin programme encourages the child to give vent to his own creative imagination and to express his own unique vision of his word-picture. I believe that the child is never more itself than in the learning method that is the Pushkin programme method.

Tom Morrow
Teacher

"...a celebration of the new self that has been born..."

Colours

Purple tastes like vimto juice.
Pink tastes like a happy day.
Blue smells like the chlorine in the pool.
Orange sounds like crackling fire.
Red sounds like a booming drum.
Green tastes like a sour lime.
Yellow feels like the hot sun.
Black feels like the dark side of people.
Grey smells like the smoke from the fire.
White feels like the sheets on my bed.

**Chiara Fiorentini, Aoife Duignan,
Tamika Bradley**
Pupils

"I found a part of me I never knew I had."

The Pushkin Challenge

I have had many memorable experiences while facilitating for Pushkin. Every Pushkin workshop is filled with moments, and each time I know for sure how absolutely brilliant the concept of blending time with nature *and* creativity is; these things together bring about a quickening in the child's – and adult's – imagination. Possibly it's simply the oxygen, the fresh air that does it – or it's something else – a connection is made – for a while at least – which enables an easier reach to the stores of ideas and creativity within. So to speak of one particular Pushkin experience that is, perhaps, more memorable or magical than others, is very difficult. Though there was this one time …

It was during the Pushkin Summer Camp, August 2010. We were at the end of a very long and full-on week – and doing the Pushkin Challenge. I can't recall the names of the teachers or children in my team, though I recall their faces. I remember, too, that we walked on a gloriously warm day through the land of Baronscourt on a route that passed three lakes. And that the deeper we went into that dark Tyrone land, the more magical the day became.

Our team was determined to win. We were clever and answered all the questions posted on our route correctly. We seemed quickly to build team spirit. No one led – but we all led. As we walked, the children began to pick up feathers and stick them in their hair; they rolled up their sleeves and trousers. Then the teachers – and I – did the same. Pretty soon we looked like the cast of *Lord of the Flies*. Further along, someone began to sing and soon we were all singing. We made up the words. We had a team song, like the work-songs of old. Suddenly our group felt like a single entity, with a wonderful sense of purpose. The happiness quotient was palpable. We could all feel it, the camaraderie, and everything on that journey felt heightened, sharpened somehow. All we had learned with Larry fell into place: we noticed animal tracks, the hoof marks of deer, the nests of birds.

When we arrived at the final lake there was a bonfire lit to welcome all the groups. The midges hovered all around the warm day. The lakewater quietly lapped the dry earth. I could see then from the faces of the children and facilitators in the other groups that they had all had the same kind of magical walk as us. Each face was lit up, each face was young.

During the walk that day, I had felt the magic and I knew I would remember it. One never knows when such experiences will strike; one has to be open to it though – for it to happen at all. And that's really what Pushkin does best; it opens the mind, heart and soul – ready to receive such moments of magic. So of all Pushkin experiences – this one – and most unexpectedly – struck deepest, perhaps because it tapped into and awakened my own childhood. I did not look for it though it certainly found me.

Jaki McCarrick
Playwright, Poet and Fiction Writer

Cycles

It has been many years since I was a child involved in Pushkin. I went to Envagh P.S. in the 1980s. Our Principal at the time, Master McGrath, was a great teacher and was always keen that we get involved in a variety of activities and competitions.

He encouraged us all to take part in the Pushkin writing competition. It is such a long time ago, but I have very fond memories of our trip to the Baronscourt Estate to take part in the Pushkin activities. I particularly remember a treasure hunt around the Baronscourt grounds. The treasure hunt ended in the front hall of the house, at a beautiful rocking horse. We gathered there for a prize-giving ceremony, at which I was presented with a book as a prize for my piece of writing. I was a very proud girl going home that day!

During my time at Envagh, we also had a visit from the Duchess and a relative from Russia. They talked to us about the origins of Pushkin and we presented them with gifts from the school. We were all given a Pushkin badge and I was given a special badge as I had taken part in the presentation, badges which I still have to this day! I also still have the photograph that appeared in the paper ... treasured memories.

Now, twenty years on, I am a teacher myself and in recent years was given the opportunity to become involved in Pushkin once again. I attended the Summer Camp of the Imagination and was able to witness the next generation of young people having fun, making friends and creating memories that they can one day look back upon with fondness, just as I do.

Claire McMenamin
Teacher

"I shall take the Pushkin ethos and methods down the years and across the curriculum in my teaching."

Partners in Education – A Tutor's Perspective

Being creative, perhaps above all in movement, is difficult.

Sometimes, in a spirit of inclusiveness, accessibility and encouragement there is a tendency to treat artistic practice as easy. Art isn't easy. If it was easy it wouldn't really be worth doing. I prefer not to undervalue it, but rather to respect its power and learn to engage well with the depth and potential of human creativity.

One way of understanding the usual level of fear and embarrassment in many participants in movement and dance is that it is expressive of a kind of hidden respect for the power of movement as an art form. The fear is stimulated by an unconscious recognition that self-conscious, creative movement practice is where we meet ourselves most directly. When we do it we face in a direct and unmediated way many fundamental issues around, for example, physicality, sensuality, disability, ageing, communication, privacy, watching and being watched.

As an educational organisation the Pushkin Trust is exceptional in the respect it gives the autonomy of artistic practice. I love to teach and have taught in many varied contexts. I do not really consider my teaching work to be separate from my artistic practice. Teaching, for me, is research. It is research into peoples' understanding of movement, into the way they understand movement as a function and as meaning. It is an opportunity to find out how people are stimulated and encouraged, how they face their fears, how they meet themselves as objective, physical beings and, importantly, how they choose to create their own 'movement poems.' This research is both reflective of and reflected in my own dance.

Taking this approach to teaching is extremely demanding on students. The general context of the Pushkin Trust and the specific context of Glenstal Abbey made it possible for the trainee teachers, their tutors and the monks who joined my dance/movement workshop to be daring and brave, to be sensitive and resonant and creative. Of course a residential weekend like this is a small input in the broader context of training teachers. However, a small pebble thrown in a large lake can produce gentle ripples right out to the edges and as any serious artist knows both 'god' and the 'devil' are in the details.

Steve Batts
Co-Artistic Director, Echo Echo Dance Theatre Company

"It is like an explorer tackling the vast outback without a map."

Roots

Roots are long and stringy
like an octopus guarding its ink
or a monster reaching out to grab me.

These roots like to worm in
and out of the ground
and wriggle around.
Roots on a river bank
tunnel deeply down into the ground
and explore for food.

If these roots could talk
they would say,
"Look how strong I am!"

They are like an
enchanted forest occupied
by honey bears and piglets.

They like to romp about,
prance around in the dirt
and play hide-and-seek.

At night these roots dream
"Will I ever get knocked over
Die and decay?"

Eimear Rogers
Pupil

A Pushkin Moment

There is an important dimension of the Pushkin experience that needs to be recognised and honoured. Because Pushkin was inspired by a belief that community conflicts needed imaginative resolutions, the teachers involved came from a broad range of social and religious groups. At the various sessions, it was most enriching to work on projects and ideas with people from such diverse traditions. Such work generated new understandings of assumptions and the roots of prejudices and revealed the shared world of feelings; of joys, of fears, of hopes that all lived in.

I can call to mind many of these experiences during my time with the Pushkin Trust. However, there is one that stands out and remains a constant reminder of how our shared humanity can be frustrated by culture and history.

There was a mature, elegant woman from a Presbyterian background whose integrity reflected the finest qualities of her faith and culture. After a couple of workshops at which she expressed her inability to write anything of value she decided to make an attempt at an autobiographical piece. After a day or so she produced a remarkable account of her childhood spent on a farm in rural Northern Ireland. In her piece she focused on the funeral of a Roman Catholic neighbour, a farmer. She recreated the sense of communal solidarity in the face of death and how that found expression in rituals of hospitality in the farmhouse where the wake was held; she described the china tea-cups and the cakes served to the ladies in the sitting room and the barrel of beer in the outhouse for the men. She remembered that as the funeral cortege moved down the driveway the herd of cattle belonging to the deceased followed it in the fields! As a child she thought that was a miraculous and wonderful sign. In her writing she recaptured all that was needed to warm and to nourish the human spirit at such a time. Having read her piece to the group she commented; "Now, such an event could not happen."

Inevitably during that Pushkin course (as on all Pushkin occasions) in the evening some socialising took place. As the evening wore on and people became more at ease, storytelling and singing started up and a most convivial atmosphere developed. As it happened I was sitting in a group with the woman who had written the piece. At some stage she remarked she was feeling guilty about being where she was. "I have never been in a bar like this before nor had an evening of singing and storytelling." Thinking perhaps that she wished to leave I suggested that if she felt that way there was no problem about her leaving, everyone would respect and understand her position. She looked at me in surprise and commented, "But that's not the problem," she said, "I love being here!"

I find it difficult to say exactly how that remark impacted on me at the time. More than likely I said, "That's great!" and got on with the evening. But now ten years on it resonates with significance.

The insight, awareness, courage and quiet desperation of that person's remark will always remain with me. She was reaching out to embrace the cultural other, the different world, and so recreate again for a brief moment the warm, communal feelings of that funeral in her childhood that had been forbidden to her by contemporary events.

That is the kind of liberating and creative experience that the Pushkin Trust has provided for myself and others. It is no mean achievement.

Tom Mullins
Lecturer, University College, Cork

Redemption

I believe in the centrality of the arts, of aesthetic experience, in our lives as individuals and as members of a community. This cannot begin soon enough – our mothers' (and fathers') knees the ideal starting place. And then there is school. I vividly recall every teacher who puffed into life the spark of creativity: Billy Greer, for instance, who led our spotty adolescence so pleasantly, as though on a country dander, through lovely work like Walter de la Mare's *The Listeners* and *La Belle Dame* by John Keats. In the sixth form at Inst Joe Cowan cyclostyles poems by W.R. Rodgers and Louis MacNeice who, literally, brought poetry home to us.

The Pushkin project is receptive, benevolent, enabling – like those excellent teachers. It recognises that although creative writing is an inner adventure which usually must remain its own reward, once in a while a little razzmatazz does not go amiss, a bit of glamour and excitement. Importantly, too, the Project salutes fine teaching. Without this priceless activity the future of the arts in our society would be even less certain. Without teachers who cherish creativity the well-being of our children would be threatened, their psychic conditions even more vulnerable to the toxins of conformity and superficiality. But the Pushkin project's chief motivation is to celebrate the vision and utterance of the young themselves. Simply and directly it demonstrates that children are worth listening to. If we listen, we may even rescue the child in ourselves. Perhaps that is what we mean by redemption.

Michael Longley
Pushkin Patron

"The Pushkin project ... removes barriers, develops respect, opens up communication and leaves a worthwhile legacy to all who participate."

Pushkin Patrons and Judges

Introduction

The Pushkin Prizes were blessed from its very inception by the support and goodwill of writers and poets from Ireland and beyond who believed in the 'voice of the child.' They likewise believed that this 'voice' should be encouraged to find creative expression in schools, both Catholic and Protestant, thereby opening new ground in which the creative spirit might take root.

I am deeply indebted to the writer [and co-conspirator!] Richard Leigh and to the educator and children's writer, Bernard McCabe who helped me build the structure and framework that was to become the Pushkin Prizes in Ireland.

The establishing of the writer as a creative role model was an integral part of the fundamental design of the project, in order that young writers would begin to see themselves in the slip-stream of the most creative and inspiring people of our time – an antidote to the then role model of the terrorist or gunman who hovered over our consciousness in the '70s, '80s and '90s.

The judges were asked not only to comment on the children's writing but also to contribute a piece for our annual Prize Day brochure by writing on some aspect of creative writing and the art of writing itself.

Now these pieces distill for educationalists and creative writers everywhere the kernels of the writing process – a veritable 'harvest of ideas.'

Sacha Abercorn

Sacha Abercorn

MAEVE BINCHY

Maeve Binchy (1940–2012) was an Irish novelist, playwright, short story writer and columnist. Her novels, which were translated into 37 languages, sold more than 40 million copies worldwide. She was regarded as Ireland's best-loved and most recognisable writer with many number one bestsellers.

"... the spray and salt air in her face, her hair wet and curling in the damp."

Almost as I Would Talk

When I started writing nobody wanted to read my stories. I never knew why this was because I was desperate to write and thought I was no worse than anyone else.

Then I set off to work abroad in a kibbutz in Israel. I wrote long letters home to my mother and father telling them about the life I was living. I wasn't trying too hard to impress them and I wasn't showing off. I was writing almost as I would talk. My father sent them off to a newspaper where they were published at once and my writing career began. I learned, by accident, that very often if you write as you talk it comes over much more naturally and people will be eager to read it.

I picked up some other rules that helped along the way. Write about what you know ... then you'll be an expert. Keep watching other people to see how they behave, and listen to them so that when you come to write dialogue it will be much easier. I'm never bored on a bus, in a railway station or in a café. Just watching and listening is the best training you can get.

And the last tip is to keep at it. Practice really does work. Write a diary, a journal, a scrapbook. Anything! Learn to type and keep it. You'll be delighted in years to come that you did.

Maeve Binchy
Pushkin Judge 1994

DERMOT BOLGER

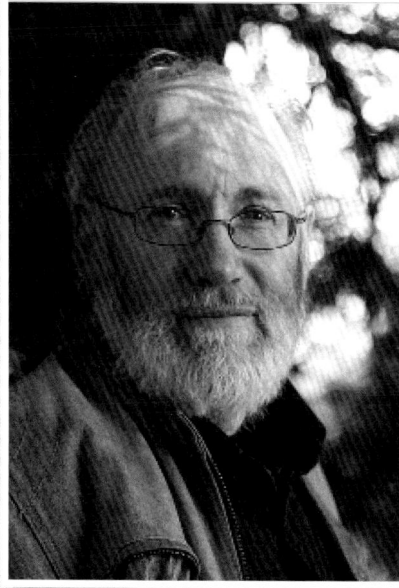

Dermot Bolger was born in Dublin in 1959 and is a novelist, playwright and poet. He has been a Writer Fellow at Trinity College, Dublin, a playwright in association with the Abbey Theatre, Dublin and a Writer-in-Residence with South Dublin County Council. He has won various awards including the Worldplay International Prize for Drama.

"... the turf embers still faintly beating like two red wings."

You Don't Need Permission to Write

Through writing you become an individual. You start looking beyond the surface to see the true good and bad within yourself, to confront both your terrors and your dreams, to express frustration, to clearly articulate love.

You don't need permission to write. There are no limits to your imaginings when you write. You are the controller of whatever university you create. In that way, being a writer is like being allowed to be a child at play forever.

At twelve I didn't know that I needed no one's permission to be a poet. I could just become one. Likewise, at twenty-two, what held me back was a lack of self-confidence, a sense that writing was some mysterious process engaged in by mysterious people. Instead it is a task which one has the confidence to stay with until you produce words that reflect something inside you of which you were previously unaware.

What the Pushkin prize does is break down that mystique. Your thoughts are important because they are uniquely your thoughts. Your words are important because they are your words. Other people may produce better words but they will never produce words that reflect you.

Dermot Bolger
Pushkin Judge 2001

SANDY BROWNJOHN

Sandy Brownjohn is a poet and a published author of
young adult books. She is also an educational consultant.
She runs writing workshops for the Arvon Foundation.
Her publications include books on the craft of the writing
process as well as children's poetry books.

*"... From clover petal tips, plucked
Like tiny pink quills ..."*

Teachers as Writers

One of the problems for teachers is that their initial training rarely confronts the actual process of writing. The aura which can surround the creative writer seems to emphasise the inspirational side and neglects to show how writers are craftspeople. As with any creative discipline, there is a kind of apprenticeship to serve, a time for learning how to use the raw materials and carve them into a honed work of art. This is why writing courses for teachers are so necessary.

Grappling with expressing one's thoughts and ideas in writing is really getting down to the nitty-gritty. By doing it ourselves we learn so much about what is possible and how to utilise this knowledge with pupils in our classrooms. Not only that, but we gain authority which comes from seeing ourselves as writers. Children will always listen to those they realise are knowledgeable in their subject area.

Teachers who attend writing courses feel a positive joy, a freedom and excitement at being asked to write creatively. They experience at first-hand the craft of writing. The magical element of inspiration is more likely to visit those who are ready and able to take it and shape it. Too often it remains stillborn.

The enthusiasm that comes from such courses arises as a direct consequence of the teachers' growing confidence in themselves as writers. This, in turn, draws out the knowledge of how to teach it with sensitivity. The pupils in their classes have everything to gain from teachers who have acquired an expertise through 'hands-on' experience.

Sandy Brownjohn
Pushkin Judge 2002

LINDSAY CLARKE

Lindsay Clarke was born in 1939 in West Yorkshire. He is a novelist. Clarke lectured in creative writing at Cardiff University and teaches writing workshops. His novel, *The Chymical Wedding*, won the Whitbread Prize for Fiction in 1989.

"... that power which conjures doves out of darkness ..."

A Particular Vision of the World

The older I get, the surer I feel of something I knew well as a child but tended to forget in the course of my education: that our sense of the world is shaped by the stories we tell ourselves about it, and that, whatever else we human beings may be, we are story-telling animals whose lives are largely made up of the tales we tell.

And precisely because stories shape our lives, it matters very much how we use our imagination in the telling of them. If we use it well our lives will feel richer, freer, more generous in their embrace; while if we use it badly, it can lock us inside stories that shadow and diminish our feel for life. For the imagination isn't only an inventive faculty, it's an ethical one too – it helps us to understand how things stand for those who live in stories different from our own, to feel compassionately with them and for them.

By encouraging teachers and pupils to flex their imaginations in ever more lively ways, and by encouraging love and respect for the language through which we tell our stories, the work of the Pushkin project must have lasting formative value in the lives of both individuals and communities.

Lindsay Clarke
Pushkin Judge 1996

ROALD DAHL

Roald Dahl (1916–1990) was a British novelist, short story writer, poet, fighter pilot and screenwriter. He has been referred to as "one of the greatest storytellers for children of the 20th century." In 2008 *The Times* placed Dahl 16th on its list of 'The Fifty Greatest British Writers since 1945.' Roald Dahl Day is celebrated all over the world on 13th September to mark his birthday.

"They is floating around in the air like little wispy-misty bubbles."

What Sort of Person must I be to become an Author?

You should have a lively imagination.

You should be able to write well. By that I mean you should be able to make a scene come alive in the reader's mind. Not everybody has this ability. It is a gift, and you either have it or you don't.

You must have stamina. In other words, you must be able to stick to what you are doing and never give up.

You must be a perfectionist. This means you must never be satisfied with what you have written until you have re-written it again and again, making it as good as you possibly can.

You must have strong self-discipline. You are working alone. No-one is employing you. No one is around to give you the sack if you don't turn up for work.

It helps a lot if you have a keen sense of humour. This is not essential when writing for grown-ups, but for children, it is vital.

You must have a degree of humility. The writer who thinks that his or her work is marvellous is heading for trouble.

Roald Dahl
Pushkin Judge 1988

POLLY DEVLIN

Polly Devlin was born in Co. Tyrone and is an author, journalist, broadcaster, filmmaker, art-critic and part-time Professor at Barnard College, Columbia University, New York. She has been a Booker Prize Judge. In 1994 she was awarded an OBE for services to literature.

"...I try to hook them up and out of the slipstream of memory into life ..."

What is a Writer?

A writer is someone who sits at a desk or a kitchen table and creates something that wasn't quite there before, as surely as does a potter or painter. You take the words and arrange them so that at the end you have an artefact – a piece of writing. And it should thicken your atmosphere. After you have read good writing you will not remain the same.

In the act of writing you change things. Writing is the image of what has been seen, and felt and loved and hoped for and dreaded and dreamed.

Writing is not talk written down although writing is all about different voices and especially about finding your own voice. There are no new stories: what is original is how you tell them.

Writing has little to do with inspiration. Writing is like bricklaying. Good writing represents years of practice, knowing what word to choose where. And *then*, then you might get inspiration. Something wonderful may happen on the page and you surprise yourself.

You have got to be able to have a feel for words, a relish for them, a sense of the strength and sinew of words, and the knowledge of how you can use them to open up your own world.

Polly Devlin
Pushkin Judge 1999

GABRIEL FITZMAURICE

Gabriel Fitzmaurice was born in 1952 in Co. Kerry. He is a bilingual poet, literary advisor, translator, teacher, musician and broadcaster. He broadcasts on Irish radio and television and has written extensively in English and Irish. He has twice represented Ireland at the European Festival of Poetry.

"... And whirling to its tune,
The dancers click their castanets ..."

Writing – Its own Reward

In writing we discover ourselves. Things we thought we believed, things we half-believed have to be discarded in the process of writing as we discover our own, individual view of the world.

Of course that won't happen just any old way. We have to refine and refine our early attempts. This is where the real writing happens. We make further discoveries about ourselves in this process if we persevere, making refinement after refinement until we are satisfied with what we have said, and with how it is said. This is hard work. But it is worth the trouble. For in the end we have come upon a truth about ourselves. Our truth. And we can live by that.

In writing there are no winners or losers. If you come to your own truth, if you express it to your own satisfaction – that is enough. No one can ask more of you. You cannot ask more of yourself. I write for the satisfaction of getting it right, of saying myself in my own community. Everything else is window dressing. For writing is its own reward.

Gabriel Fitzmaurice
Pushkin Judge 2001

AUBREY FLEGG

Aubrey Flegg was born in Dublin and was a geologist before he became a full-time writer. He won the Peter Pan Award 2000 for his first book, *Katie's War* and *Wings Over Delft* won the Bisto Book of the Year overall award in 2004.

"The new-mown hay
lay in silver ribbons in the fields."

The Restless Traveller

Writers have to imagine the people for whom they are writing and it is under the supervision of this imagined reader that I write my first draft. In fact he or she does not interfere, but leaves me to my own devices. I look out of the window. I dream dreams. I chase ideas as if they were butterflies. I even churn out stuff that I know is no good just to get it out of the way. Sadly the dam-bursts of ideas and images that appear on paper turn out to be as incomprehensible to others as were my artistic efforts when I was a child.

So, I gaze again at my first draft, which now looks more like an explosion than a manuscript. Hasty scribbles are connected to unfinished sentences by looping lines; chunks that might be prose nestle like nuggets between cluttered margins. Whether we feel like gardeners turning the wilderness into a place of beauty, or like rangers cutting paths in the jungle for our readers to follow, our role is to turn the jungle of our first drafts into something other people can understand so as to bring our ideas to safety, and, in the process, travel to places where no one else has been. It is worth every hour, every mile.

Aubrey Flegg
Pushkin Judge 2002

BRIAN FRIEL

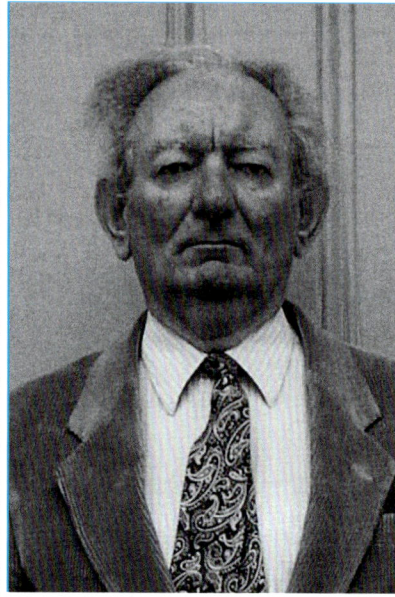

Brian Friel was born in 1929 in Co. Tyrone. He is an Irish dramatist and author. He is considered to be one of the greatest living English-language dramatists, hailed as an "Irish Chekhov." Friel has written more than thirty plays and has been elected a Saoi of Aosdána. His plays have been a regular feature on Broadway.

"... to whisper private and sacred things, to be in touch with some otherness ..."

Literary Virtues –
Valuable Signposts for the Teacher

Good writing must first of all be accurate writing. Good writing must be exact and precise and efficient. Nothing comes between the eye and the object. No nudging comments. No spurious emotion. No bogus concern. Just exact and precise and efficient telling. So I would suggest that writing lessons in school might concentrate much more on that type of exercise. Describe the shoes you are wearing. Describe your biro. Describe your mother's hair. Only when the writer has acquired the skill to recreate real objects and felt experience, only then can he or she attempt to describe what he or she imagines or sees in his or her mind.

Children have very active imaginations. A talking buttercup is as real as a trip to the seaside. So that when we speak of children's imaginative writing what I would suggest is that pupils be encouraged to apply the same stern discipline to imaginative writing as they do to 'ordinary' writing. If a story is about a rabbit that uses contact lenses, make that make-believe real and accurate. The premise of a fiction does not relieve the writer of the responsibility of writing factually. Indeed if the fiction is not realised, the fancy is betrayed.

Brian Friel
Pushkin Judge 1989

FRANK GALLIGAN

Frank Galligan is a writer, broadcaster and journalist. He is a former N.I. Chairman of the UK National Year of Reading and has researched extensively on the historical links between Ireland and the birth of bluegrass music in the U.S.

"For our slow airs and easy graces."

Liberating Language

We cannot teach someone – child or adult – to write. We can, however, demonstrate how spontaneity can be usefully channelled, thus ensuring disciplined creativity; and how imagination is all the more effective when it elicits in the mind of the reader, either 'I wish I was there', or 'I think I was there.'

Finding one's own voice takes time and patience but ultimately the strength of that voice will decide which genre – either poetry or prose. In 1822, Pushkin defined the virtues of prose as "exactness and brevity." Yet, his first major work, Eugene Onegin is a "novel in verse," described by Gogol as "Brilliant, exact and free." The supreme achievement of Pushkin's poetry is its willingness to meet prose.

The child must be allowed to explore all genres, to marry prose and verse, to experiment with styles beyond definition, to realise that somewhere in the tension between exactness and freedom, spontaneity and discipline, lies the indefinable quality which creates great literature.

Frank Galligan
Pushkin Judge 1994

CARLO GÉBLER

Carlo Gébler was born in Dublin in 1954. He is a novelist, short story writer and playwright. In 2009 he was Royal Literary Fund Fellow at Queen's University, Belfast and in 2010, Writer Fellow at Trinity College, Dublin.

"The ground was scattered with pearls of wet."

Striking the Right Note

Before beginning to write wait until you know you're full with something and only then start to work. If you're not ready and you force yourself, your writing will not strike the right note. It will seem, somehow, like an instrument not pitched properly.

When you write, work slowly. This is easier said than done. If I can I remind myself that rushing always produces a mess and it is better to get one thing done that's done right than ten that are wrong.

When I have finished writing something I put it away in a drawer and I do not let myself look at it for days or even weeks. When I get it out again I will then see it with fresh eyes. I will know without thinking what is right about what I have written, what to keep and what to cut.

Carlo Gébler
Pushkin Judge 1995

MARIE HEANEY

Marie Heaney was born in Co. Tyrone. She trained as a teacher and received a Master's Degree in Irish Studies. She has compiled and edited books for both adults and children and writes for television and newspapers. She lives in Dublin with her husband, the poet Seamus Heaney.

Creative Writing in Schools

I remember vividly my first bout with creative writing in schools. It was around 1950 and I was a pupil in a primary school in rural Tyrone. When I next encountered creative writing I was fresh out of college and teaching in an Intermediate school in Co. Down. I discovered then what a sound job my old teacher had done. I tried to do the same, encouraging the children to find the best words they could to describe what they had seen and felt, and to get into their writing some of the energy of the actual moment.

As a teacher, I knew the imagination was at work when I read a piece of writing that was true and satisfying and could have been written only by that child in those circumstances. At such times the child's satisfaction was obvious too. It is satisfaction, and the confidence it engenders, that makes creative writing so beneficial for school children. None of them may become writers. Most of them will never write again after they leave school but for a while they will know something of a writer's satisfaction as they make sense out of confusion, put order on things beyond their control and create something of their own that cannot be taken from them.

Marie Heaney
Pushkin Judge 1990-1993

SEAMUS HEANEY

Seamus Heaney was born in 1939 in Co. Derry in Northern Ireland. He has published poetry, criticism and translations. In 1995 he was awarded the Nobel Prize for Literature. He has been a Patron of the Pushkin Trust since 1987.

"Now strike your note ..."

Trust in Potential – Impatience with Cliché

I am proud to have been associated with the Pushkin Prizes from the outset and know how much the work they encourage means to all who participate in it. At an intimate, personal level, the writing of a poem or a short story becomes a kind of growth ring within the life of the individual who writes it: it marks time in many senses and gets remembered as a significant stage in the growth of that person's inner freedom and self-esteem. At an institutional level, moreover, the sponsorship of such valuable inner development adds inestimably to the achievement of a thorough education, connecting the emotional and the intellectual development of the child in a uniquely integrated way.

The message emanating from the Pushkin Prizes is therefore very much one that we want to hear not only at the end of the first decade of their history, but at the end of the second millennium of our era. It is a message in praise of creative joy and psychic integrity, of trust in potential and impatience with cliché, a call to everybody to be more ardently and originally themselves.

Seamus Heaney
Pushkin Patron

FRIEDA HUGHES

Frieda Hughes is an English-born Australian poet and painter. She has published seven children's books and four poetry collections and has had many exhibitions. She became an Australian citizen in 1992. Hughes is the daughter of poets Sylvia Plath and Ted Hughes.

"... his face a lantern
In the light of all that colour ..."

Flexing the Imaginative Muscle

Young children of four or five have imaginations limited only by their lack of experience and the number of words they know in order to tell you what they see. As we get older, we learn more words, but we also find more to distract us. The distractions pull us down and ground us so we don't float away.

A vivid imagination is a gift and we all have it. Some of us feed it and exercise it and some of us let it sleep in front of the television or playstation, locked up in a cage that is no bigger than the box in front of us.

Being able to make words on a blank piece of paper conjure up an image or an incident that wasn't there before, is magical. It is a combination of talent, imagination and the use of your experience, your knowledge and your vocabulary. You might be very talented and imaginative, but if you do not sit down and work nothing happens. On the other hand, you might not have a great deal of talent and imagination, but you might be able to extend your abilities and make up the distance by sheer dogged determination which in turn will stretch the muscle of your imagination and make it work brilliantly for you.

Frieda Hughes
Pushkin Judge 2000

TED HUGHES

Ted Hughes (1930–1998) was born in Yorkshire. He is considered one of the twentieth century's greatest English poets. Over a forty-one-year writing career he won numerous prizes including the T.S. Eliot Prize for Poetry, the Whitbread Prize for Poetry, and the Whitbread Book of the Year twice. In 1984 he was appointed England's Poet Laureate.

"Has slipped through a fracture in the snow-sheet ..."

A Word about Writing in Schools

Before the pen moves over the paper, the writer's imaginative re-creation of what is to be written must be (as near as this is possible) as if real. The life within the words, the anatomy of sentences, and the music of narration or argument, can be taught, and must be taught. But how can such a thing as strength and steadiness of imagination be taught? Most teachers simply assume that the faculty is weak or strong by nature, and nothing can be done about it. Yet few teachers doubt that in writing, and in English Studies generally, a strong imagination is a pupil's greatest asset. It will do most of the English teacher's work spontaneously. If only it could be taught, and taught early, and strengthened and trained throughout school life, many a problem would be avoided without much further effort.

Without some training of this faculty, we waste most of our time teaching writing – except to the very few. With the help of this training, and a wise use of it, we find a surprising thing: a large proportion of any class have rich potential as writers.

Ted Hughes
Pushkin Judge 1989

BENEDICT KIELY

Benedict Kiely (1919–2007) was born in Co. Tyrone. He was a novelist, short story writer, journalist, broadcaster and lecturer. He received the award for literature from the Irish Academy of Letters and in 1996 was elected a Saoi of Aosdána in recognition of his contribution to literature.

"The Slieve Blooms have gone back into the mist which is really the evening."

Some Guidelines for the Teacher

Keep your eyes and ears open for people and places; listen to folk and to stories; keep a notebook.

Then your mind will begin to work on the realities around you and your imagination will add colours and details.

My father said; "Never spoil a good story for the sake of truth." He didn't mean that you were to go around telling lies, rather, let imagination work on reality and it may or may not become more real.

Benedict Kiely
Pushkin Judge 1992

JOAN LINGARD

Joan Lingard was born in Edinburgh in 1932 but grew up in Belfast. She is the internationally renowned author of more than twenty novels for young people and twelve for adults. She received the prestigious West German award the 'Buxtehuder Bulle' in 1986 and was awarded an MBE in 1998 for services to children's literature.

"… the first smudges of pale pink light in the sky …"

The Ring of Truth

As a child growing up in Belfast, I was crazy about books. I read and read and could never get enough to read. And why did I read so much? Early on, it seemed to me that life was limited: you could lead only one life, inhabit one body, one mind. By reading one could enter into other worlds, inhabit other people's skins and minds. Books pushed out the boundaries of existence and made one's own world seem wider.

I was eleven years old when I sat down and began my first novel. It was about smugglers, and I set it in Cornwall (where I'd never been), and I think, if you read it, you'd have said at the end I was under the influence of Enid Blyton. I didn't write a single word about Belfast when I was young. I thought 'You can't set books here!' Faraway places always seemed more exciting. I know now that it's better to write about familiar people and places – unless it's fantasy of course – for then your story will be more believable. It will ring true. And that is one of the things one requires of a story: that ring of truth.

Joan Lingard
Pushkin Judge 1993

MICHAEL LONGLEY

Michael Longley was born in Belfast in 1939. He is a poet. He has won the Whitbread Poetry Award, the T.S. Eliot Prize, the Hawthornden Prize and the *Irish Times* Poetry Prize. In 2008 Michael Longley was appointed Ireland Professor of Poetry and in 2010 he was awarded a CBE.

"Gorse fires are smoking, but primroses burn ..."

Peddling this Benign Narcotic!

The moment of inspiration is like a stone breaking water's calm surface. The disturbance, the commotion results in a lovely pattern of ripples. The ripples are the shape of the poem. Today we are all like fisherman's floats bobbing in the ripples that continue to radiate from Pushkin's moments of inspiration, from his great poems.

By far the most exciting experiences that I know are, first of all, the moment of inspiration and then the concentration involved in the following through on that initial buzz, and being led into the unknown places. The hours fly by: the hours pass like minutes.

We want to get young people addicted to these two excitements. Teachers of English (and Irish) should be peddling this most benign narcotic – the magic of language, the liberation of self-expression, the thrill of sharing our words with others. Poetry provides an oasis where we can choose a few words for ourselves and try to make sense of things on our own.

The writing that moves me reflects the young authors' experiences and has its roots in their everyday speech. I am able to visualize what they describe and I hear in my head their voices talking to me candidly as individuals. They seem at home in the world, at ease with their five senses. They have the courage to be themselves.

Michael Longley
Pushkin Judge (1995) and Pushkin Patron

WILLIAM TREVOR

William Trevor was born in 1928 in Co. Cork. He is a novelist, playwright and short story writer. He is widely regarded as one of the greatest contemporary writers of short stories in the English language. He is a member of Aosdána. He has won the Whitbread Prize three times.

"Moments and the mood of moments make up that distant childhood."

Good Writing is a Subtlety

When writing your task is to make something out of nothing – to find the words and the way to communicate them so that your fascination with your subject equally fascinates the reader. It's a tall order, but then anything worthwhile is.

Even if you decide that you don't want to go on creating something out of nothing, to use words in a style of your own, even if words do not become, as it were, your business – remember they'll always be there and you'll have to string them together. Ahead of you there are letters that will have to be written: letters that apply for jobs, letters that argue your case when you have a point to make, CV's that state your achievements and qualifications. And you'll reach out for the words that are perfectly the right ones to do justice to your skill in persuading, to make the most of expressing yourself. Do not despise what may seem to be mundane: good writing in whatever form is a subtlety.

William Trevor
Pushkin Judge 2000

MARTIN WADDELL

Martin Waddell was born in 1941 in Belfast. He writes children's books. He may be known best for the texts of the picture books the *Little Bear* series. For his "lasting contribution to children's literature," Waddell received the biennial, international Hans Christian Andersen Award in 2004.

"Little bear played bear-tricks-with-bear-sticks."

A Writer's Insights

It is important to recognise that the development of an individual voice as a writer is crucial. You can't teach 'voice,' because it is peculiar to the individual. You can wait to see it happen and cheer wildly when it does or, point out when it is missing. If writers can be persuaded not to say what qualities someone possesses but to show the qualities, either in dialogue or action, a huge improvement results.

A sense of place does not mean using place names, or explaining what they mean. It is the feel of the place which is important. I think this can be achieved by the use of small detail or the description of some emotion relating to the place.

I would like to see all children encouraged to think very carefully about the opening sentences of their stories, bearing in mind that a story with a dull beginning usually remains unread. The reader must want to read on and to find out more.

Good writing is about finding a voice of your own, a distinctive way of saying ordinary things in a manner which makes them extraordinary.

Martin Waddell
Pushkin Judge 1990

GERARD WHELAN

Gerard Whelan was born in 1957 in Co. Wexford. He is the author of many books for children and has won the Eilis Dillon Memorial Award for first-time writers and the Bisto Book of the Year Award in 1998.

"... the sweet air of the summer night brought in a scent of distant greenery."

Imagination is the Key

Creativity is a wild thing, and a contrary one, and hard to objectify for long enough to define. For one thing, creativity per se can't really be taught at all. To teach something you have to understand it in some sort of logical fashion, and creativity, being wild, and illogical in the true sense, cannot (by definition) be understood logically. All teaching requires rules, but the 'rules' of creativity are not fences to keep out what lies beyond, but obstacles to be tested from within. Not only are they there to be broken, but the rate at which they're successfully broken is in itself an index of progress.

Every child is creative. The task for the teacher, or anyone else who could encourage this creativity, is to locate and nurture it and – when the rules come into it – show the child why they are important. They are not meant to be off-putting stumbling blocks, deterring the child from experiencing the pleasures of that socially accepted form of telling whopping great lies which we have named creative writing.

The distinguishing mark of good creative writing is imagination. Succeed in encouraging that, and the rest will follow.

Gerard Whelan
Pushkin Judge 2000

Pushkin Judges

The Pushkin Trust would like to acknowledge the inspiration of the entire cohort of Pushkin Prize judges between 1988–2002.

1988	Roald Dahl
1989	Ted Hughes
	Sam McAughtry
	Brian Friel
1990	Doris Lessing
	Marie Heaney
	James Simmons
1991	John Banville
	Marie Heaney
	Martin Waddell
1992	Benedict Kiely
	Marie Heaney
1993	Marie Heaney
	Joan Lingard
	Joanna Lumley
1994	Maeve Binchy
	Frank Galligan
	Marita Conlon McKenna
1995	Michael Longley
	Orla Melling
	Carlo Gébler

1996	Lindsay Clarke
	Leon McAuley
	Eilís Ní Dhuibhne
1997	Irina Ratushinskaya
	Michael Scott
	Anne Dunlop
1998	Medbh McGuckian
	Jill Pirrie
	Tom McCaughren
1999	Polly Devlin
	David Park
	Paula Meehan
2000	William Trevor
	Gerard Whelan
	Frieda Hughes
2001	Dermot Bolger
	Gabriel Fitzmaurice
	Adele Geras
2002	Sandy Brownjohn
	Marilyn Taylor
	Aubrey Flegg

The Pushkin Trust would like to acknowledge the generous support of its Funders

Department of Education NI

Department of Education ROI

AIG

An Chomhairle Ealaíon

American Ireland Fund

Area Development Management Ltd.
(Programme for Peace and Reconciliation)

Arts Council NI

Arts Council ROI

Arts for Nature Trust

Atlantic Philanthropies

AWB Vincent

Baron Woods

Bord na Gaelige

Barrow Cadbury Trust

Bryan Guinness Charitable Trust

Calor Gas

Castellini Foundation

Charles & Ann Johnson Foundation

Co-operation Ireland

Coca-Cola

Desmond and Sons Ltd.

D'Oyly Carte

Esmée Fairbairn Foundation

Esme Mitchell Foundation

Enkalon Foundation

Eranda Foundation

Fredrick Paulsen

Fischer Trust

First Trust Bank

Foras na Gaelige

Forward Emphasis

Friendly Brothers of St. Patrick

Fyffes Group plc

Irish American Partnership

J Paul Getty Jr

James Mellon

John Jefferson Smurfitt Monegasque Foundation

The Pushkin Trust

Baronscourt, Newtownstewart, Co. Tyrone, BT78 4EZ, Northern Ireland.

e-mail: info@pushkintrust.com   web: www.pushkintrust.com